*SOMETHING
VENTURED
SOMETHING
GAINED*

SOMETHING VENTURED SOMETHING GAINED

A Business Development Guide for Nonprofit Organizations

LAURA LANDY

ACA BOOKS
American Council for the Arts
New York, New York

Copyright © 1987, 1989 Laura Landy

No part of this publication may be reproduced by any means without the written permission of the publisher. For information, contact the American Council for the Arts, 1285 Avenue of the Americas, 3rd Floor, New York, NY 10019.

Editing by Joan Stevens and Bruce Peyton
Jacket design by Celine Brandes, Photo Plus Art
Book design by Robert Porter
Printing by Gagne Printing

Director of Publishing: Robert Porter
Assistant Director of Publishing: Sally Ahearn

94 93 92 91 90 89   10 9 8 7 6 5 4 3 2 1

ISBN: 0-915400-81-2

Printed in Canada

CONTENTS

ACKNOWLEDGMENTS vii

1 INTRODUCTION 1

2 SETTING THE SCENE 5

3 THE VENTURE PLANNING PROCESS 11

4 EVALUATING THE ENVIRONMENT FOR A BUSINESS VENTURE 15

5 VENTURE GOAL SETTING 25

6 EXPLORING AND EVALUATING BUSINESS IDEAS 31

7 PRELIMINARY FEASIBILITY STUDIES 43

8 THE FULL FEASIBILITY STUDY 49

9 EVALUATING THE TAX CONSEQUENCES OF EARNING MONEY 59

10 FUNDAMENTALS OF MARKETING 71

11 PRO FORMA FINANCIAL STATEMENTS 77

12 THE BUSINESS PLAN 87

13 FINANCING OPTIONS 93

14 THE BUSINESS PLAN - A DETAILED RESEARCH
    AND PLANNING GUIDE 103

15 PARTING ADVICE 133

    BIBLIOGRAPHY 137

    ABOUT THE AMERICAN COUNCIL
    FOR THE ARTS 143

ACKNOWLEDGMENTS

I would like to extend my sincere thanks to several individuals and organizations whose belief in the nonprofit sector and in the value of creativity, enlightenment and experimentation make ventures, including this one, possible. I'd like particularly to acknowledge Joan Stevens, whose patient editing made this volume accessible to the reader; Vivian Beetle, Rosemary Bruner and Hoffmann-LaRoche Inc. for providing financial support; Judith Trachtenberg and the Center for Non-Profit Corporations for their vision and commitment; Robert Porter at the American Council for the Arts for his support and hard work; Professor Zenas Block and the staff of the Center for Entrepreneurial Studies at New York University's Stern School of Business for keeping me challenged and current in my knowledge of corporate venturing and entrepreneurship; my many clients and students who have taught me so much; and my husband, Robert, whose love and support has made many things possible.

I'd like to dedicate this volume to a very special person, our little daughter, Juliane Rose, who was born while this book was being written. She has already taught us much about life. We owe her a better world to grow up in.

Laura Landy

1 INTRODUCTION

This book has been written as a guide for the nonprofit organization interested in undertaking a business venture. In recent years, nonprofits have increasingly looked to earning money as a means of supporting their operations. Income-generating ventures have ranged from selling greeting cards, to providing home health care services, to major manufacturing operations. The common motivation has been the continued ability of the nonprofit organization to deliver services.

This growing trend has taken place during a period of decreased governmental support and increased competition for charitable contributions. At the same time, private sector businesses have increasingly invaded territory considered by some to be the domain of the nonprofit sector. And nonprofits, many of which have begun to compete with small business, are facing tighter controls on their income-producing activities.

For some, the business venture still appears to be the solution to the problem of providing a stable income stream to the nonprofit organization. For others, venturing represents risky, unfamiliar and unappealing activity.

The purpose of this book is to present a realistic introduction to venturing, the potential risks and repercussions, and the philosophical and practical issues involved. The book describes a step-by-step process through which the nonprofit considers its suitability for pursuing a business, evaluates the environment for an income-generating venture, researches business ideas, and develops a detailed business plan. It is a conservative process, a logical process, and a process that will not be totally unfamiliar to most nonprofit organizations.

Nonprofits considering a business venture today can benefit from the experiences of other organizations, both nonprofit and profit making. There are many successes and failures from which to learn. The fifty-fifty success-to-failure ratio is the same whether the venture is undertaken by a nonprofit or by a profit-making business.

The chapters that follow are based on six related assumptions:
- The nonprofit organization is seriously interested in undertaking a venture and in doing so in a sound and businesslike fashion.
- The nonprofit is interested in earning a substantial amount of money, an amount significant to the organization and its ability to provide services.
- The nonprofit is more important than the business idea or the individuals behind it. A choice between damaging the nonprofit or the business will always be made in favor of the nonprofit, its integrity and continued well-being.
- The primary objective of the venture is to earn money, or at least break even. While the venture may further the mission of the nonprofit and certainly must not conflict with that mission, the specific mission of the organization for this particular activity is most often secondary to the goal of earning money. The income generated will be dedicated to the nonprofit.
- The nonprofit will be associated with the venture for an extended period of time. The venture is not a one-time event, but an ongoing operation providing a dependable source of income to the organization over many years.
- The nonprofit organization believes in its ability and is willing to undertake the challenge of starting a business venture.

For some nonprofits, it may be realistic to expect the venture to be a major or sole source of support to the organization. This may be true where instituting a fee-for-service operation accomplishes the specific mission of the nonprofit. For most nonprofits, however, the venture will represent only a small part of the funding portfolio. In a recent study conducted by the Center for Entrepreneurial Studies at New York University, nonprofits predicted that 10 to 15 percent of their revenues would be venture income by 1990. The current percentage of venture income for most organizations is less than 5 percent.

Five or fifteen percent is a significant portion of the budget of most nonprofit organizations, but it will not replace fundraising events, foundation proposals or government contracts. Venture income can provide the nonprofit a degree of freedom and flexibility because the funds have no strings or commitments. The money can be used to support overhead costs, to experiment with new services, to leverage funds from traditional sources, to underwrite core programs out of vogue with the funding community, or to raise salaries, and thereby keep first-rate staff.

For other nonprofits, the venture may represent a means of advancing the organization's mission. The business may provide jobs to clients or provide services to a new client population. A business venture can enhance the nonprofit's reputation, increase its visibility and improve fund raising.

Planning and developing a successful business venture may take twelve to eighteen months. It is a serious commitment of time, energy and resources, but it is an opportunity well worth exploring.

2 SETTING THE SCENE

A business is a process of exchanges. In a business transaction, goods or services are exchanged for some form of consideration. That consideration can be cash, other services or other products, but without the exchange there is no business. A business involves a direct exchange.

Many nonprofit organizations receive grants from private foundations or from government agencies. In accepting a government grant, for example, the nonprofit is obliged to provide a stipulated service to a client population. This is not a business exchange because the government receives nothing in return for underwriting the cost of client services. The diagram in Figure 2.1 shows that both the money and the service flow in one direction. At no time is there a direct exchange. The government does not pay for services it receives, nor do the clients pay for services they receive. In this situation, the nonprofit agency acts as an extension of the government, as an agent, by delivering services the government chooses not to provide itself.

In another example, the government contracts with the nonprofit organization for a particular service that the government wishes to receive, such as conducting an environmental assessment of a proposed new road.

FIGURE 2.1: Not a Business Exchange

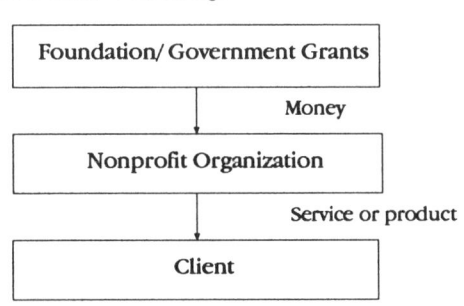

This would be a business exchange. Or, if a client pays the nonprofit for a service he or she receives, this would be a business exchange.

A venture is an ongoing business activity conducted by an established nonprofit or profit-making organization that introduces new or existing products or services into new or existing markets (Figure 2.2). A venture normally requires changes in the way the organization operates, whether it be changes in management, staffing, marketing, financing or other operations. A venture is risky because it is new and different from the organization's previous experience.

For the purposes of this book, when we talk about businesses and ventures, we mean direct exchanges of products or services for cash or some other consideration. In addition, the business ventures under consideration are planned to operate in a market without subsidy. The business will be planned without low interest loans, without free or reduced cost labor, without free rent. The business will be planned on the basis of the true market economy. Otherwise, success of the business is dependent upon decisions outside the control of the organization.

The typical nonprofit organization considering a business venture has probably been operating for ten, twenty, fifty or more years. During this time, it has established a presence and positive reputation in the community. The organization has created reliable systems and attracted a quality staff. In place are a committed staff, a strong board, sound programs, management systems and fundraising mechanisms. The organization has its own ongoing demands and requirements.

And now the nonprofit is considering undertaking an activity that differs substantially from its previous experience—starting a small, growing business. The business venture will have demands and requirements of its own. The venture may require different financial systems, different marketing mechanisms, different capitalization, a different board and different staff with different compensation needs. The business will also require support from its nonprofit parent in order to grow.

The leadership of the nonprofit organization will have two responsibilities: operation of the ongoing organization, and development and operation of the new and growing venture. At times these two operations can be compatible and supportive, which increases the chances for success. But at other times the two operations will be in direct conflict: the needs of one may undermine or damage the other. The potential for conflict is evident in the characteristics of the two operations.

The characteristics of an established, well-managed and respected nonprofit corporation include the following: an established, respected and active board; stable management; a stable, qualified staff; delivery of quality services; established financial, personnel evaluation and management infor-

FIGURE 2.2: Forms of Venture Activity

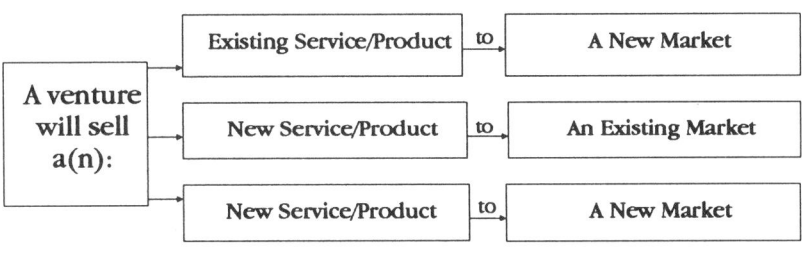

mation systems; established means of communicating to clients and the public; an established short-term and long-term planning process; and a relatively stable budget. The nonprofit has a clearly defined mission, an established corporate culture, shared values and a committed staff. The established nonprofit has a financial history, which serves as a basis for independent evaluation and planning. There are internal approval and communication systems in place. The established nonprofit organization concentrates much of its effort on building and maintaining the loyalty of its existing clients.

In contrast, an entrepreneurial venture is driven daily by its need to succeed. The venture has no track record on which to base its plans or to be evaluated. The primary focus is sales: to attract customers, to make sales, to cover costs and to produce more goods. The new venture has few, if any, systems in place because there is little time to develop systems and because systems seem unnecessary in a small operation. The small staff is hard working, and driven by a need to succeed or a desire for financial gain. There is a high tolerance for risk and uncertainty. Planning horizons are short, decisions are made quickly and changes are implemented rapidly. The board has to be small, accessible and immediately responsive.

Funds are insufficient, cash flow is tight and the ability to predict current cash flow or income is limited. Evaluation is constant but nearly always informal. While the established nonprofit is based on systems and predictability, the entrepreneurial venture is based on a lack of predictability and a need for flexibility.

When the established nonprofit and the new venture operate side by side, or one within another, the potential for conflict is obvious. The differences between the nonprofit organization and the business venture are those described in the business literature as the differences between a mature corporation and a growing corporation.

Business theorists describe the evolutionary stages of a business in the *business life cycle:*

- In the first, the *conceptual stage,* the idea of the business is conceived and researched.
- During the second stage, the *developmental stage,* the plan for the business is developed.
- The business is started and begins to grow during the third *growth phase.*
- As the business continues to grow, it enters the *mature stage.* The mature business goes from a lack of systems to the creation of systems, from limited to greater delegation and from generalized skills to specialization and division of labor. The mature business is not stagnant but growing at a slower rate.
- During the *decline stage,* the market activity decreases and, if nothing is done to resurrect it, the business dies.

Each stage of the business life cycle makes different demands of management. When a nonprofit organization undertakes a business venture, the existing system strains to meet the demands of the mature business (the established nonprofit) and the demands of a growth business (the entrepreneurial venture). The mature nonprofit wants control of the venture to protect its resources and track record from risk. The growth venture wants flexibility and freedom from control systems. By imposing systems appropriate to a mature business on a growth business, the parent nonprofit may impede or prohibit the success of a venture.

For example, a hypothetical nonprofit organization decides to start a business selling green plant rental and maintenance services to major corporations. The nonprofit has not yet made its first sale but has been courting one corporation for some time. This first sale is a milestone, a key event

FIGURE 2.3: The Business Life Cycle

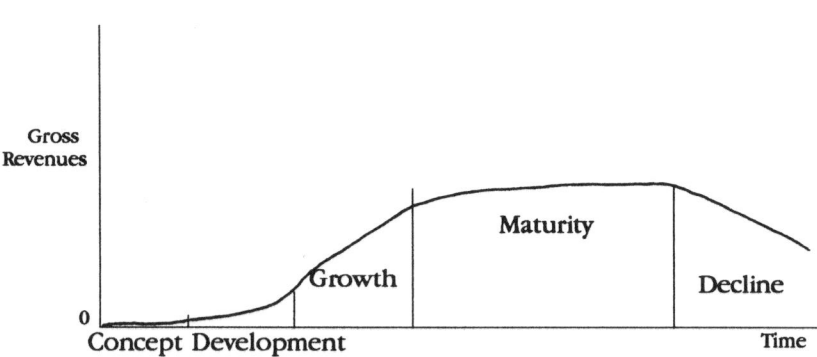

necessary to the establishment and growth of the business. The potential client is not pleased with the price and makes a counter-offer: instead of the $150 monthly service charge presented by the nonprofit, the corporation will pay $100 per month during the first year and then evaluate the arrangement. The nonprofit's venture manager is satisfied. They will barely break even, but it is a well-known corporation and a first client. It is a chance to demonstrate the venture team's abilities, establish a track record and have an important, visible reference.

However, the manager has to follow the nonprofit's established process by clearing the counter-offer with the organization's finance director, the executive director, possibly the board's finance committee, executive committee and full board—a process that could take two months or more. This process, which is common to and effective for nonprofit organizations, may unintentionally sabotage the new business. The corporation may choose not to wait and decide to hire a competitor or do it themselves. The manager must have the flexibility to make immediate decisions. Systems that hinder the manager's ability to function hinder the ability of the business to succeed.

To protect themselves, nonprofit and profit-making parent organizations often impose systems that smother fledgling businesses. The desire for information and control must be exercised in a manner that satisfies the needs of the parent corporation but allows the fledgling corporation the freedom it needs to succeed.

The business literature on new ventures reveals an interesting statistic that may illustrate the controlling influence of the parent corporation on new businesses. The average business started in the United States by an individual achieves profitability in approximately four years. However, ventures started by corporations take an average of nearly eight years to achieve profitability. While other factors, such as venture size, amount of capital and level of risk may account for some of the time differences, requirements imposed by parent businesses do retard growth and development of new businesses.

The parent corporation can do more than delay business growth. Recently, a major bank started an investment banking division as an internal venture. The investment banking division was very successful, its employees were earning high salaries and large commissions and wanted additional capital in order to expand. The managers of the parent corporation, a conservative commercial bank, saw the venture as a threat to the established corporate culture. They saw that the investment banking division could detract from the bank's traditional activity. Besides, the new investment bankers were earning more money than the commercial bankers. In response to the request for increased capital, the parent corporation closed the investment banking division, rather than confront and address the value conflicts that had emerged.

A successful venture initiated by a nonprofit organization can similarly threaten the culture of the parent nonprofit. In order for a venture to succeed, the parent organization must be committed to the venture and motivated to see that it succeeds. That commitment may only come from the belief that the long-term survival of the nonprofit depends upon a successful venture.

3 THE VENTURE PLANNING PROCESS

This book describes a ten-step venture planning process for nonprofit organizations:

Step One: Develop a strategic plan for the nonprofit organization that evaluates the need for and goals of a venture.

Step Two: Evaluate the suitability and impact of a business venture on the nonprofit organization and its environment.

Step Three: Establish goals for the business venture.

Step Four: Explore business ideas and opportunities.

Step Five: Evaluate potential business products and services.

Step Six: Conduct preliminary feasibility studies.

Step Seven: Conduct full feasibility study.

Step Eight: Write business plan.

Step Nine: Obtain financing.

Step Ten: Start the business.

Some steps in the venture planning process are described in greater detail in this book than are others. For example, the book devotes a chapter to the legal constraints and possible tax consequences for a nonprofit organization undertaking a business venture. This subject, but one aspect of the feasibility plan, merits extra attention. Another chapter introduces some marketing issues helpful in preparing the feasibility study and business plan.

Other steps in the process are subjects requiring their own books. The final step, starting the business, is left for another volume. And, the first step, strategic planning, is discussed only briefly below.

By following the steps in the venture planning process, the nonprofit systematically selects, designs and learns how to operate a business before actual operations begin. By learning from others of their successes and failures, we are able to reduce costly on-the-job training that results in so many business failures and significantly increase the chances for venture success.

STRATEGIC PLANNING

The strategic plan for an organization analyzes the organization's history, activities and environment and then projects where it will be in three, five or more years from the present. The plan outlines the actions and resources necessary to reach these stages and the obstacles that must be overcome to move in that direction.

The strategic plan is a key factor in determining the nonprofit's need for a business venture, the desirability of a venture and the form the venture might take. The venture must be viewed as an integral part of the strategic plan and must support, not detract from, accomplishment of the organizational goals.

The strategic plan also serves as the foundation for selling the venture to the nonprofit board and staff. The strategic plan projects the income potential of various sources, the revenue needs to support future programs and the estimated funding gap. These projections are a legitimate basis upon which to explore alternative sources, such as an income-generating venture. Without this kind of research and rationale, nonprofit boards of directors and staff often see ventures as unnecessary, risky and unrelated to the main function of the organization. The strategic plan can demonstrate how a business venture and the income it generates are related, and possibly essential, to the future of the nonprofit organization.

The process of preparing a strategic plan assists the nonprofit in clarifying its mission, its objectives and its target population, as well as its underlying values and corporate culture. As a result of this process, the nonprofit is in a better position to define the kind of income-generating venture fitting the organization. Would it be appropriate to charge fees for services? If fees are acceptable, must they be low for broad accessibility or can they be as high as the market will bear? Are there program areas with fee potential that could subsidize other programs? Could some individuals be charged higher fees in order to subsidize low or no fees for other clients? What other sources of income have been explored as part of the strategic plan? How might a business venture support the overall plan for growth and development?

The strategic plan may present other reasons for undertaking a business venture such as capitalizing upon an existing relationship with another service organization, instituting a new service or serving a new client population. A business venture might take advantage of underutilized volunteers or corporate contacts for other than fundraising purposes. The strategic plan might identify underutilized assets, such as space or equipment, with venture potential.

Strategic plans often strengthen the underlying structure and systems of the nonprofit—the personnel system, the financial system, the management information system and other reporting systems. The reinforcement of these systems provides a firmer foundation on which to build a venture.

The strategic plan can be formally or informally prepared by the nonprofit. However, the issues raised during the strategic planning process must be addressed. Without the proper foundation of a strategic plan, the chances of a successful venture are diminished.

4 EVALUATING THE ENVIRONMENT FOR A BUSINESS VENTURE

Chapter Two described important differences between a mature corporation and a new corporation, and the differences between a nonprofit and a profit-making venture. These differences alone may raise serious concerns. Unlike many businesses, the nonprofit faces different, often conflicting, challenges in its daily operations. Among these are the dual requirements of raising funds and providing services. While these functions may be closely related and mutually supportive, this is often not the case. The management systems required for these two sets of activities may co-exist but without the close integration one would prefer. One element of the staff may be responsible for raising funds, and another staff element responsible for providing services. It is hoped that there is good communication between the two elements; however, this is not always easy to achieve. An agency sometimes may be driven by the kinds of funds available, rather than by priority of services. This may cause dissent within the organization. Or those responsible for funds may be less familiar with the services than those providing the services feel is necessary. These two management systems need to communicate with each other and to provide mutual support.

Beginning a business venture adds a third and totally different management requirement to the nonprofit organization. The organization will still have to be concerned with traditional fundraising because ventures are projected to raise only 10 to 15 percent of nonprofit budgets. The organization will still have to manage the delivery of quality services. And now it will be responsible for the sale of a product or service in what may be a totally new market.

This will be a new and exciting challenge. But before diving into entrepreneurial waters, it is important to anticipate and plan for the reactions of those who may see the venture as a potential threat and those who may see it as a positive opportunity. The nonprofit wants to minimize the threats and to capitalize on perceived opportunities. The objective is to anticipate and control events, not to be diverted from starting the venture.

In evaluating the environment—the nonprofit and the larger community it serves—the organization may discover reactions too severe or too negative to allow implementation at this time. There may be a great deal of groundwork to be covered even before raising the idea of a business venture. The venture may be inappropriate for the nonprofit simply because support is nonexistent. It is far better to discover early in the venture process, before spending $30,000 or more on planning and preparation, that the necessary support does not exist.

A large social service agency on the East Coast took more than three years to develop the internal support necessary to begin serious exploration of a business venture. The board, board committees, executive director and staff members explored ideas, opportunities and the venture concept. Only after three and one-half years were the key players comfortable enough to engage a consultant to work with the agency in looking at the idea more seriously. The process was slow but necessary if the venture was to succeed.

Key to the success of this agency's venture was the role played by two individuals who were the "champions" of the idea of a business venture. These two individuals, holding senior positions in the agency's management structure, were committed to the value of undertaking a venture. Without their persistence and the groundwork they laid, the venture would have died an early death within the organization.

THE VENTURE CHAMPION

For any venture, the existence of a committed champion is a necessary requirement. Without the commitment of an individual or team of people, support will never grow, work will not proceed and the venture will not succeed. The champions believe the venture is the right direction for the organization and is critical to the organization's survival. Whatever the composition of the champion group, it is essential that it exist. The champions should be able to maintain their support throughout the planning, initiation and operation of the venture. The champions require the access necessary to build support for the venture. They need to know what needs to be done and to take the action necessary to move the venture ahead. It is, to be sure, a politically sensitive role.

The significance and sensitivity of the championship role varies with the size and risk the venture represents to the nonprofit. The larger the organization and the greater the venture's risk, the stronger the reactions one can anticipate. For these reasons, often it may be better to start with a small venture or with several small ventures. The risk is limited and financial investment is minimal. The organization can build on the experience of these small successes before attempting a larger scale venture. Whether an organization is ready for a sizable venture to generate substantial income, or for a minor venture as a trial for a larger business, it is critical to examine the positive and negative impacts of the business venture on the organization and its surrounding community.

THE MONEY VS. MISSION CONFLICT

Perhaps the greatest fear among members of the board of directors and the staff is that the original mission of the nonprofit will be lost in the effort of the business venture to earn money. This has been called the "money vs. mission" conflict. There are serious concerns that clients will be lost in the shuffle, that the quality of services will decline and that the integrity of the program will be undermined. This problem can be avoided by having a clear vision of how the venture fits into the overall operation and future of the organization. To say a venture cannot overwhelm a nonprofit is to ignore instances where this has happened. However, for each example of this kind of injury to a nonprofit, there are several examples showing substantial benefit from the venturing process.

An extreme case of a venture overwhelming the mission of a nonprofit organization is the case of a venture started by a youth program in the Bronx several years ago. The venture idea was to start an herb garden that would sell fresh herbs to local restaurants and gourmet groceries in and around New York City. The herbs were to be grown in the South Bronx, packaged and distributed, and the income returned to the youth program. The nonprofit received a great deal of attention and financial support in its effort to initiate this venture. A corporate executive was loaned to the nonprofit to manage the venture. So much time and attention were invested in establishing the business that insufficient time and attention were devoted to the relatively small youth program behind the venture. The venture became very successful but overwhelmed the youth program. The youth program was closed, and the venture was sold to the loaned executive, who left the corporation to run the venture on a full-time basis. As a result, the South Bronx had one new thriving business but one less youth program.

The nonprofit's loss to the venture might be attributed to the instability of the nonprofit, or to the more rapid growth of the venture than the nonprofit or, perhaps, to the excitement generated by the success of the business. It should be noted that one of the goals of the venture was to provide job opportunities for clients of the youth program, and this was accomplished.

Examples of successful ventures where the mission of the nonprofit has not been undermined are varied: the design, printing and sale of napkins by a Midwestern Jewish community center; the operation of a small art gallery by a San Francisco community theater; a gourmet food repackaging business operated by a rehabilitation agency in upstate New York; the operation of gift shops within museums; the well-known sales activities of National Geographic and the Sierra Club; the operation of a restaurant by a California religious organization; the development and management of retirement housing communities by church groups; and the operation of a coffee house by a small dance company. Within the health care industry, business ventures range from collection agencies to home health care operations and laundries.

The threat to the mission of the organization lies more in the need to maintain balance than in the nature of the venturing process. The new activity offers a challenge that can kindle excitement and growth for the total organization.

The balance of this chapter examines five constituencies within the nonprofit organization and their possible reactions to the idea of initiating a business venture. In this review process, the nonprofit should think about the people it knows and works with, attempt to anticipate their negative and positive reactions, and plan a strategy for minimizing negative impact on individuals and the organization and for maximizing positive responses.

THE BOARD OF TRUSTEES

Boards of trustees of nonprofit organizations tend to be conservative. Even people who are personal and professional risk takers tend to assume a more conservative stance when they join a nonprofit board. It may be a heightened sense of social responsibility, a sense of fiduciary responsibility for the organization's assets, or a lack of understanding about how their risk-taking abilities and business skills can serve the nonprofit organization. Board members serve for a variety of personal, professional and community motivations. Their conservative nature may be attributed to individual qualities or to the goals of the organization.

Whatever the composition of the nonprofit board, nothing is surer to elicit strong reaction than suggesting a business venture as a source of income for the organization. The range of concerns and questions are likely to include the following:

- Why is the nonprofit starting this business venture?
- Who will manage the venture?
- What qualifies a nonprofit manager to operate a business venture?
- To what kind of liability will the venture expose the organization?

- To what kind of liability will it expose individual board members?
- What happens to the nonprofit if the business fails?
- What happens to the board member's reputation if the business fails?
- Where will the nonprofit obtain start-up capital?
- Where has this been done successfully?
- Are board members no longer responsible for raising funds from friends, corporations or foundations?
- Will the nonprofit lose its tax exempt status?
- Will the nonprofit lose major contributors if it goes into business?
- What will the nonprofit's funders say?
- Will grants to the nonprofit decrease if it earns money on its own?
- Who on the staff will plan this venture and get it off the ground?
- Is it legal for a nonprofit to do this?

At the same time, board members may respond positively to the venture idea. Board members often see ventures as an opportunity to provide stable income to the corporation. They may see the venture as an opportunity to apply their business skills and make a contribution they felt unable to make under the organization's current structure. The venture may increase the nonprofit's visibility, enhance its viability in the community or augment its ability to raise funds. Board members may see the venture as an opportunity to differentiate the agency from other organizations in the community. They may see the venture as a means of increasing staff salaries or providing new job responsibilities to individuals who might otherwise leave. Some board members may suggest contacts that will help in the development of the business. Others may identify possible sources of capital or provide the funds themselves. It is not uncommon to see both negative and positive reactions within a board or even from individual members.

The nonprofit must do its homework. It must anticipate questions and be prepared to answer them before announcing the venture idea. The announcement should be gradual, perhaps over lunch with key board members, and nonthreatening. It should provide a link to the strategic direction of the agency, a general overview, an understanding of what is and what is not possible, what the role of the board members might be, and what the organization has to gain from such a venture.

It is recommended that a committee of board members, possibly supplemented by persons with particular business skills from outside the organization, be responsible for overseeing the venture planning and for making recommendations and reports to the full board. The committee will provide a focused group to work with management on the development of the venture. Board members will be able to raise their questions and concerns with this committee. Having board members talk to other board members is often more effective than having staff talking to board members on a controversial issue.

THE STAFF OF THE NONPROFIT

Members of the organization's staff may be very enthusiastic about the venture idea. Some of their interests will be similar to that of board members. The venture is a chance to test new skills, to generate funds and to do something that has not been done before. It is an opportunity to serve clients in a new way, or to gain resources necessary to expand the nonprofit's services in an area of particular interest. Management and development staff may see an opportunity for developing new contacts, for expanding the agency's focus, for providing better quality services, or for an easier means than traditional fundraising.

On the other hand, like the board, staff may feel threatened. They may see the agency shifting focus and wonder what will happen to the values on which the organization has been built. They may worry that the culture of the organization will change dramatically and that they will not fit in the new scheme. They may foresee a shift in the focus of top management with more emphasis on the venture and less on standing operations. They may be concerned that they as individuals, or their programs, will no longer receive proper attention and will suffer as a result. Staff members may feel they are not qualified to staff the new venture and worry what will happen to them.

Someone accustomed to providing a social service free of charge may feel uncomfortable with the idea of requiring payment. Staff members may challenge the value of a service that was unquestioned as long as it was free but may seem of less worth if someone must pay for it. This can become a substantial issue for individual staff members.

The venture represents change within the organization, and any change brings discomfort. The venture may require different kinds of staff and different kinds of people. A homogeneous group of social workers, for example, may be dismayed by a business school graduate in their midst.

It is reasonable of board and staff members to ask whether the nonprofit has the right team in place to undertake a business venture. This is particularly true if the venture will require the work and support of existing staff. The nonprofit may need to hire new staff, and the new staff need to understand that the organization is going in a new direction.

Similarly, the nonprofit may need to replace board members or add new board members with particular business skills, attitudes and understandings about where the organization is headed. Once a venture has been introduced in a nonprofit, it is not unusual for several board members to resign. Many board members, as well as staff members, are committed to the traditional operation of the organization. The venture represents a potential threat to tradition and to organizational stability. These changes may be desirable—in fact, necessary—if the nonprofit is to thrive.

THE CLIENTS OF THE NONPROFIT

The clients served by a nonprofit organization are an important constituency to be considered, particularly if the venture introduces fees for the first time. Charging fees where no fees were charged before radically changes the dynamics between staff and client. The client becomes a customer. As customers, the clients have a choice: if they are going to spend money, where do they choose to spend it? The clients become empowered and their ability to reject the nonprofit affects revenues. Staff perceptions and responsibilities may change with payment: if clients are paying, staff must provide more of what they want, not what staff members think they want or need.

Introducing payment for services may require a change in attitude among staff providing services and staff providing management support. Altruistic paternalism within a nonprofit is less appropriate in the context of consumer choice. There is the story of a senior citizens agency that served lunch to a number of its clients. The clients had been coming for some years and seemed satisfied with the service and quality of food received. The agency decided to institute a minimal charge for the lunch, a dollar or less per day. Over the next several weeks, fewer and fewer clients came until only one or two were coming for lunch. Finally, a meeting was called of the senior citizens who had been patrons of the lunch program. After a lot of discussion but little communication, one woman stood up and said, "When the food was free, it was fine. You know I like coming here. I don't like you any less. But if I am going to pay for my food, I would rather go to the church down the street. They have a better cook, they have a better menu, and it is sure nicer paying a dollar to eat there than to eat here." The nonprofit's dilemma was either to shape up their menu and provide better food, or to establish a lower-price or no-price lunch program. Otherwise, they had lost their entire client group.

Clients may also become concerned if they see the focus of the agency changing. They may fear that commitment to their cause may be diverted to other matters: the quality of services or the amount of time devoted to them will be reduced. Clients are particularly important when they serve on advisory boards or on the agency's board of trustees. It is important to acknowledge their fierce self-interest, their belief that the nonprofit exists solely to serve them. They may have a limited perspective on what is needed for the organization to survive and continue to provide services in the future. However, they may have a valid perspective on how changes in the organization will affect services traditionally provided.

Clients may see the business venture as an opportunity for expanded services, for reduced fees or for job opportunities. Client concerns will differ depending on the type of nonprofit organization and the nature of the venture. An arts organization may be concerned about the reaction of its audience to a change in pricing policy, a change in program or serving alcoholic beverages in the lobby before a performance. An educational program might be concerned about the reaction of existing clients to a diversification of its clientele. An environmental group may have relatively few concerns about client reactions. A social service agency intimately involved with its clients may be concerned about the emotional and psychological impact of certain changes.

Clients may provide great market opportunities and often represent the sole market for expansion of products or services. The Metropolitan Opera Guild has raised more than $11 million annually through the sale of memberships and products, primarily to audiences of the Metropolitan Opera in New York. Their clients are not an obstacle, but their market opportunity and the Guild's concerns are those of any marketer trying to sell a new product or service.

FUNDERS OF THE NONPROFIT

The funders of the nonprofit organization are a fourth constituency to consider. Funders may be great supporters of the venture idea. They may become a source of capital for planning the business venture or of start-up funds for its operation. On the other hand, some funders, particularly government funders, have provisions in their contracts to reduce their grants by every dollar that is earned. Funders may see the venture as an opportunity for terminating support. Other grant-making organizations may see a potential source of administrative problems for themselves because they are unsure how or what they can do to support a business venture.

It is important not to alienate key supporters or traditional sources of funding. No matter how successful the venture, it will not replace all funding sources immediately, and probably will never do so. Maintaining existing relationships is critical to continuing services during and after the venture is established. The nonprofit should talk with its funders, understand their concerns and answer their questions. At the very least, their concerns should be acknowledged in the planning process.

Major contributors require special attention. Individual conversations with major contributors and the leaders of giving campaigns are recommended. Their concerns and questions should be considered before moving ahead aggressively.

THE SMALL BUSINESS COMMUNITY

Finally, it is important to consider small businesses in the local community. In recent years, there has been an increasing amount of nonprofit activity in the marketplace. Many of these activities have been challenged by small business owners who believe they are subject to unfair competition coming from the nonprofits. They claim that the tax exempt status of the nonprofit organizations, lower postal rates, subsidized overhead costs, access to cheaper capital and the relationships of nonprofits to captive markets provide the nonprofits with advantages not normally available to the small business community. Most of the protests to date have come from particular industries—health care, university testing and laboratory services, computer sales, hearing aid sales and travel agencies. Many of those challenging the nonprofits belong to the Business Coalition for Fair Competition. This coalition has worked with the U.S. Small Business Administration to attract attention to what they see as an unfair situation. Several legal cases have challenged the right of a nonprofit organization to maintain its tax exempt status while operating a business venture. A YMCA has lost its exemption from real estate property taxes through a challenge from a private health facility. It was claimed that the YMCA was operating essentially a commercial health club where prices, facilities and location were virtually identical to those of a commercial operation. This was judged not in fulfillment of a charitable purpose; therefore, the real estate tax exemption was inappropriate. Now under appeal, the case has attracted a great deal of attention.

In another case, a hospital in Utah lost its tax exempt status when its operation was found to be essentially the same as the operation of a private for-profit hospital. The 1986 federal tax law changed the tax exempt status of certain nonprofit "commercial type" health insurers, such as Blue Cross and Blue Shield, formerly totally nonprofit corporations.

Members of the small business community claim that tax exempt organizations are unfairly using their advantages to compete in the marketplace. Nonprofit organizations argue that they are only charging fees in order to generate revenues to pay for those services or other activities consistent with their missions. This is an important issue for nonprofits to follow carefully.

What is more important for the nonprofit organization considering a business venture is to evaluate its local small business community. What is the venture under consideration and from where might potential challenges come? Is it realistic to expect such challenges? Might a partnership or collaborative effort diffuse potential conflicts? Would a challenge from the small business community lead to political consequences beyond the business venture and endanger the organization's ability to raise funds and operate in the community?

The extent of dissatisfaction or challenge to nonprofit ventures is unknown, as are the economic and market impact that nonprofit ventures have had. The cry of unfair competition raised by the Small Business Administration and by the small business community has challenged the right of nonprofits to function in the marketplace. The U.S. Congress is examining tax laws dating from the 1950s to see if they are appropriate for the structure and activities of the nonprofit sector today. What nonprofits can do, what they will be taxed for and what kinds of subsidies they are eligible to receive may come under greater scrutiny at the federal level.

These issues may also become the subject of state and even local legislation. For example, some state legislatures have passed laws favorable to subcontracting of government services to nonprofits. Other states have said that services may be contracted to the nonprofit sector or to another government agency only if there is no private sector firm capable of providing the services. One state prohibits nonprofits from using their funds to invest in for-profit ventures.

The issue is very political, and how it will be resolved remains to be seen. In the meantime, the nonprofit organization should know its community, know the reactions to anticipate and try to avoid areas where conflict will result.

FINAL EVALUATION

After evaluation of the venture environment, the nonprofit organization is at a decision point, the first of several during this process. Is your nonprofit corporation in a position internally and in relation to the external community to pursue a business venture? Are there constraints that must be imposed on the venture in terms of size, visibility or activity in order to avoid conflicts that might be detrimental to the organization? Are there actions that must be taken to prepare the staff, the board or the community for the introduction of the venture? If the nonprofit is not an appropriate organization for the venture, now is the time to stop before further investment of time, energy and money. Without the support of the board of trustees and without the visible leadership of a champion, a venture has little chance of success.

5 VENTURE GOAL SETTING

Once the nonprofit organization has positively evaluated the environment for a business venture, the next step is to establish goals. This must be a clear statement agreed to by the board, the staff and others intimately involved in the decision making about the venture. The statement should specify what the organization expects the venture to do, what the venture will contribute to the parent organization and any constraints that must be imposed on the venture.

Goal setting creates an environment for discussing the venture idea before discussing specific business activities. It allows people to talk about what they are doing, why they are doing it, what they want it to accomplish and how it fits into the organization as a whole. The consensus-building and support-building process enables people to talk strategically about the venture concept without getting sidetracked by the pros and cons of a specific venture project. Goal setting allows people to question the venture concept, to raise board and staff concerns and other issues that must be considered before moving ahead.

In addition, goal setting provides clear guidelines for the types of ventures to be considered, how they will be selected and how they will be managed. The venture goal statement guides the rest of the process and provides a standard against which to evaluate venture ideas. At important points in the process, participants can ask, "Does this venture meet the goals the organization is trying to accomplish?"

In setting goals, it is necessary to consider the broadest range of reasons a nonprofit organization or group of individuals within the organization would consider initiating a business venture. It is important to be honest in order to be sure that the goals of the venture reflect reality.

The range of motivations can be broad, and motivations are not always what they seem to be. The first motivation most people identify for starting a venture is money, but money alone probably is insufficient. For what purpose is the money needed? Perhaps it would enable the organization to increase staff salaries or to expand services to a particular population.

A different type of venture goal may be to provide new and exciting activities for staff members, the executive director or deputy director, who may be growing bored with their duties and responsibilities. Other possible goals might include the following: providing access to new markets; developing new contacts useful in fundraising; providing greater visibility to a program in order to expand services or fundraising; providing specific products or services to advance the organization's mission; or providing services or products not directly supportive of the organization but capable of generating extensive income.

Personal goals may be among the motivations for starting the venture. A successful venture might allow the project champion to leverage success into a new job elsewhere. Some individuals may be motivated by the desire to start a business, something they have been afraid to do on their own but for which they see an opportunity within the organization. Personal motivations are not necessarily negative. They may provide the interest and support to make the venture a success.

Goals may be broad, such as reaching a new client population or developing a new service that cannot be subsidized otherwise. Or goals may be narrow, such as creating jobs or financing a mortgage or building repairs. Some motivations are sufficient for starting a business; others are not. In any case, it is important to start by listing all the primary or secondary benefits of the venture.

After identifying all the motivations for starting a business venture, the next step in goal setting is to quantify and assign priority to items listed in the goal statement. The goal statement should include: the dollar amount to be generated by the venture; the time period in which the money will be generated; the uses for which the money will be allocated; and, any constraints on the venture. Examples of constraints might include: "We do not want to be in the food industry," "We do not want to be in competition with the chairman of our board," "We want to stay away from travel businesses because of charges of unfair competition," or "We do not want to invest more than $50,000 in capitalizing the business."

Finally, the goal statement might include growth criteria, for example, "We want a venture with potential to grow 20 percent a year." The goal statement should be realistic, helpful in attracting support, and provide the organization with direction in making decisions so the business venture moves ahead. The goal statements of three fictional nonprofit organizations are examined below.

Organization One. The goal of Organization One is to raise $10,000 to pay for building repairs to expand an existing program into currently unusable space. They want to accomplish this goal within one year and have no other constraints on the venture.

Organization One's goal is to earn income to support a relatively modest one-time capital expense. There should be a way to raise the funds necessary to repair the building that is easier and faster than a venture, which may take several years to plan, start and operate. The effort required of a business venture could be devoted to a capital campaign or other fundraising project that would take advantage of the skills and network familiar to the nonprofit. It makes more sense for Organization One to raise the needed funds in a traditional manner rather than look to a business venture as a source of income.

Organization Two. The goal of Organization Two goal is to establish an independent business with a growth potential of at least 15 percent per year. The venture should break even in three years and generate a profit of no less than 10 percent per year thereafter. They hope to generate at least $25,000 profit by the end of the fourth year. Profits would be devoted to other program activities. The venture should provide transitional employment for fifteen persons with disabilities working side by side at equal pay with non-disabled employees. Organization Two wants to invest no more than $75,000 in the establishment of the business, and the venture should be located within two miles of their current operation.

Organization Two has a goal statement that involves providing jobs for clients and generating profits. Within its goal statement, the organization has defined its market—a business that can operate locally, a business that can serve clients and a business that is compatible with the skills and ability of clients. In doing so, the organization has limited the kinds of businesses it can consider. There are constraints on the kinds of tasks certain persons with disabilities can perform. The business may have to take into account limitations on activity and special quality control needs. There may be limitations on the kinds of chemicals or machinery to be used. Supervision and training needs may be different than they would be for a non-disabled work force. Defining the work force and the business location may narrow the options for the kind of business that can be considered.

Two elements in Organization Two's goal statement may potentially be in conflict: the employment of fifteen clients with disabilities and earning $25,000 in profits. A business employing workers with certain disabilities may be more expensive to operate than others in the industry. Higher costs for training and quality control may limit profitability. It may be possible to employ clients and to make a profit, but it may be difficult to do so.

Organization Two must decide which is of higher priority, making maximum profit or employing certain clients. The nonprofit must be prepared to make the decision: Does it employ workers with disabilities and possibly foreclose or limit profit, or does it select only non-disabled workers in order to generate maximum income? Generating $25,000 or more in profits may enable Organization Two to provide greater benefits to its client population than employing fifteen clients in the business venture. A choice must be made between potentially conflicting priorities. The first priority must be established before the business is operational. Otherwise, Organization Two can anticipate a crisis in its venture.

Organization Three. After an eighteen-month start-up period, Organization Three wants to generate $35,000 per year. The income earned would support overhead and staff salaries so the nonprofit could expand its programs for populations now underserved.

Organization Three's goal is to provide additional income to support services. Options are available to Organization Three that may be foreclosed by the limits set forth by Organization Two. Organization Three may choose a related business that breaks even, covering only the costs of overhead and salaries for the expanded services. Or it may choose a business unrelated to the organization's mission and services and generate income to pay the costs of the nonprofit's expanded activities. It is necessary to examine the services provided by the organization, their market potential and the organizational impact of expanding services, as well as some of the profit-making options, before making the final decision of which business is most appropriate. Simply instituting fees for services may meet the organization's goal, which several counseling agencies have achieved by offering services within affluent communities where higher fees-for-service can be charged. Staff, working part-time in this community, earn higher salaries as a result of the higher fees charged.

The goal statement adopted by any nonprofit organization helps in evaluating what size operation and what kind of business venture makes sense. How much profit is needed or anticipated from the venture? Profit is the amount of money remaining from the business operation after subtracting all expenses. It is most important to consider *all* expenses, not just the direct expenses. Otherwise, the true cost of the business is underestimated, as are the risks and viability of the venture.

Profit is often evaluated as a percentage of business volume. Industry ratio tables, available at a business library or through the local Chamber of Commerce, show the average profitability of different kinds of businesses in the United States. Profitability ranges from a low of one percent in the grocery store/food industry to as high as 50 percent in certain service industries. For an average business, after expenses and before taxes, profit is seven to eight percent of the total sales volume. In order to generate a 7.5 percent profit of, say, $30,000, a business must have approximately $400,000 in sales. This is a serious, full-time business operation. It is important to understand the level of commitment and obligation necessary to build an operation of this size. A venture that provides income directly to the nonprofit, as opposed to generating income for the nonprofit through profits, will obviously not require this level of activity to generate $30,000. However, other constraints will be imposed, including limited unallocated cash. If a nonprofit organization is not prepared to make the effort necessary to build sales at this volume, now is the time to re-evaluate goals, re-evaluate the environment and consider other options.

If achieving sales of $400,000 feels feasible within the specified time period, the organization is ready to start selecting its business product or service.

6 EXPLORING AND EVALUATING BUSINESS IDEAS

There are thousands of business ventures that a nonprofit agency, or private corporation or enterprising individual, might possibly pursue. These range from running a gas station to organizing young people to perform services for businesses or individuals; from housing management to corporate day care; from running a laundry service to selling T-shirts or mugs at dance concerts; from opening a retail gift shop to selling computer software. Each idea has the potential for success. What is important is whether the idea is an appropriate match between the nonprofit and its skills, and the needs of the marketplace.

Your potential customers are individuals and corporations—nonprofit, public and private. People never buy something they don't need. Like most cliches, this is true. At the moment of purchase, the individual believes he or she needs the item enough to pay money for it. The sellers of the product or providers of the service must help the consumer to recognize the need for their product and must encourage the consumer to purchase it from them.

The need for a product or service may be a basic need, such as food, clothing, housing, new materials or machinery. Or it may involve a less vital need related to status, competition or the desire to feel attractive. Needs vary according to socioeconomic standing, ethnic background, educational level, place of residency, stage of life and gender.

Every need of a certain population represents a potential market niche. The successful venture gains a foothold in the market by targeting a specific product or service to the needs of a certain segment of the population.

A second cliche deserves attention: no risk, no return. Before venturing into the marketplace, the nonprofit organization must recognize that without risk there is no return. Investors in new businesses, called venture capitalists, expect only one to two percent of the businesses in which they invest to be successful. The odds are about the same for business ventures undertaken by nonprofits. Only one, maybe two percent, of all the venture ideas they will consider will be good businesses.

At the same time the nonprofit is seeking a venture idea that matches its skills and resources with a market need, the organization must realize that the business environment requires some risk. The nonprofit can minimize risk by building its venture on an area in which it possesses knowledge and experience.

BRAINSTORMING BUSINESS IDEAS

Brainstorming business or product ideas should involve a small group of staff or board members and, perhaps, some carefully selected outsiders. The group should understand the goals of the organization and be committed to the process of working through business ideas. They should be open to exploring possibilities and should be responsible in selecting those ideas that make sense.

The goal of the brainstorming session should be to come up with 100 to 150 possible venture ideas. Many will be ridiculous; some will be inspired; others will be mundane. From a list this length, it should be possible to find a few ideas worthy of further pursuit.

FIGURE 6.1: Identifying Business Ideas and Opportunities

```
┌─────────────────────────┐      ┌─────────────────────────┐
│ Assess nonprofit skills,│      │  Assess market trends,  │
│ experience and resources│      │    technology, and      │
│                         │      │      environment        │
└───────────┬─────────────┘      └────────────┬────────────┘
            │                                 │
            │                    ┌────────────▼────────────┐
            │                    │ Assess needs created by │
            │                    │ trends, technology and  │
            │                    │      environment        │
            │                    └────────────┬────────────┘
            │                                 │
            │    ┌─────────────────────┐      │
            └───►│ Match needs with    │◄─────┘
                 │ skills and resources│
                 └──────────┬──────────┘
                            │ result
                 ┌──────────▼──────────┐
                 │ Possible business   │
                 │    opportunities    │
                 └─────────────────────┘
```

Some participants will think they have already identified the perfect business idea. One of these "perfect" ideas may be the best idea for the organization. On the other hand, there may be other ideas or variations that offer more potential with less work or less risk. Members of the brainstorming group will have a tendency to believe their own ideas are best. Maintaining objectivity about what is a good idea and what is not a good idea, from a business perspective and from a market perspective, is very important. Is there a demand for this product or service? Does it meet a real need? Is the need sufficient that people will pay for it, and in big enough numbers, to meet the goal set by the organization?

ORGANIZATIONAL RESOURCE INVENTORY

By sticking close to home and basing the business venture on skills and resources within the organization, the chances of failure are greatly reduced. This enables the nonprofit to build upon an existing base rather than starting from scratch.

The nonprofit should start brainstorming by making a thorough inventory of the skills and resources available within the organization that could provide the basis for building a business. These resources will be much broader than expected.

People resources include staff, board members, clients, major donors, funders, government, suppliers, parents, families and volunteers. Careful examination of each of these groups may reveal potential production workers, potential consumers of goods or services, or a potential sales force. Among these people may be the knowledge base needed to organize the venture, important market contacts or a financing source.

In evaluating people resources, it is important to examine the whole person, not just the way he or she is known within your organization. Staff members may have skills and experience from previous jobs that may be a basis on which to build a business. They may have hobbies and hidden talents, ambitions or needs that may provide the basis for a successful business venture.

There are other resources within the organization that could provide an opportunity for a nonprofit business venture. The inventory should examine underutilized resources, such as unused staff time or facility space that is not used full-time. Equipment may be idle some of the time, or it may have been purchased for a now defunct program and no longer used at all. The nonprofit may have program experience that can be translated directly into a business opportunity. Certain services or products might be priced more effectively or marketed more efficiently. Products used internally within the organization may have market value. These include training programs, manuals and resource guides. The nonprofit's management system, software system or management information system may be marketable to other organizations. Experience with a client population may be sufficient for establishing a venture, perhaps serving a more affluent group of the same population.

The way the nonprofit operates may lend itself to particular opportunities. Do people come to the facility often? Who are they and why do they visit? This might be a sales opportunity. For example, a performing arts group has a large audience coming regularly to a particular site. In addition to the ballet performance, this might be an opportunity to sell tours to see dance in other countries, to sell T-shirts or used toe shoes, to sell refreshments, to offer cocktail party or dinner packages before or after performances, to offer tours of the facility or a chance to meet the stars. All these ideas are based on the identification of an opportunity—people coming to a specific place for a reason. How can the organization take advantage of that opportunity?

The geographic location of the organization may be another business venture resource. The Museum of Modern Art in New York sold the air rights above the museum to a condominium developer. This may have been a unique opportunity, but the benefits of the location should not be ignored.

Patents and copyrights are another basis on which a business may be built. The patent-worthy invention may have been created within the organization, or it may be donated to the organization by a friendly contributor, board or staff member. Materials and reports may be a source of venture activity.

Programs and activities should be broken down for their component parts. The operation of a summer camp means that you have skills in recreation planning, nutrition and food service, landscaping, building maintenance, transportation, marketing, etc. Each alone is the basis for a venture, as is the whole. This survey of possible resources does not represent an entire list of starting points for a venture, but it demonstrates the range of resources already available to the organization. What is needed is a thorough inventory of what is available to the nonprofit.

TREND ANALYSIS

The next brainstorming step is to develop a more complete understanding of trends and moods in the community and the larger society. This can involve pulling together casual thoughts and information gleaned from community involvement and from reading local newspapers, national papers and magazines. The objective is to identify emerging trends that will grow over the next five to ten years. Whatever business venture the nonprofit plans to undertake must consider the long term.

EXPLORING AND EVALUATING BUSINESS IDEAS

For example, planning a business based on the Cabbage Patch doll craze probably makes no sense at this point. But understanding the success of the Cabbage Patch dolls can be helpful. Increasing alienation experienced as a result of the proliferation of technology in our society, some suggest, leads to the desire by adults and children alike to form close relationships with animate or inanimate objects. If this is an accurate rationale, the trend will increase as society becomes more technological. This has been characterized as the "high tech, high touch" phenomenon.[1] For every new high tech invention on the market, there is something soft and cuddly to counter the high tech impact. What might you do to satisfy this need?

Trends provide a wide range of opportunities. What is happening in the local real estate market? What kinds of businesses are moving into the area or moving out? Are there services or products required by the new businesses or by those relocating? Where is major new development planned? Is the development residential, industrial or commercial? What are the implications of these changes for business opportunities or for other trends?

The nonprofit needs to understand the demographic trends in the community it serves. Is the population getting older so that services for senior citizens become more important? Are many young families moving into the community so that services for children become increasingly important? Are there transitional neighborhoods where people constantly move in and out? Are neighborhoods changing in terms of homogeneity, income levels or educational levels? These trends have implications for possible service needs.

Life-style trends are another factor to be considered. How is the potential market for a business idea influenced by the trend toward two-worker families? Will the roles of men and women continue to change, and in the same direction? If so, what kinds of services or products might be required as a result of such changes? Are there implications of an increase in leisure time? Does the aging of America affect the organization's community and the possible products or services it might provide?

Attitudes toward health and fitness have shifted radically in recent years. Will this trend continue and what are the implications if it does? Will scientific discoveries such as relationships between cholesterol and heart disease or nutrition and cancer affect dieting decisions and change the way people live? How will the AIDS epidemic affect society and what kind of products or services may be required?

There may be market niches in countertrends to the basic trends. For example, while the nation as a whole has become more diet conscious, a cola product with double the sugar and caffeine of a normal cola drink has

---

[1] Naissbitt, John. *Megatrends* (New York: Warner Books, 1982), pp. 39-53.

been marketed successfully. The drink has appealed to college students who want to stay up late or choose cola instead of coffee in the morning. Another marketing opportunity might be to provide services to the still large number of women not employed outside the home.

After the nonprofit has completed its resource inventory and trend analysis, the organization is ready to begin brainstorming ideas that match resources with market needs. The process should be open, creative and free-wheeling to get ideas on the table for later evaluation.

PRODUCT DEVELOPMENT MATRIX

The product development matrix, a standard marketing tool found in most marketing textbooks, is very helpful in structuring the brainstorming to assure that new approaches and opportunities are considered.

We start by understanding and inventorying all the products/services and markets/relationships the nonprofit has now. These are represented in the upper left-hand corner of the matrix below. We then will build on the base to develop a new opportunity.

In developing a new product or service idea, there are two basic options: sell an existing product or service or sell something new. Similarly, there are two basic market options: sell to existing consumers or clients or sell to somebody new. These options are represented on the matrix.

FIGURE 6.2: Product Development Matrix

PRODUCT OR SERVICE / MARKET	EXISTING	NEW
EXISTING	Market Penetration	Product Expansion
NEW	Market Expansion	Diversification

Theoretically, the nonprofit can reduce the risk of its venture by building upon either existing relationships or building on existing products and services. These are four options the organization can consider, beginning with the boxes on the matrix labeled "existing." The first option is to sell an *existing* service or product to an *existing* market. This is called market penetration. If the goal is to make a $10,000 profit, this might be accomplished by simply doubling the volume of current activity. Through increased income and economies of scale, the organization might be able to make $10,000 without changing what it does or to whom it sells. For example, a nonprofit makes a small profit marketing a housing magazine to advocacy groups. It sells to only 5 percent of the housing groups in the country. If, through increased marketing, it could reach 10 percent or 15 percent of the housing groups, it may make the extra $10,000 it seeks.

Market penetration would require an increase in the number of units sold. This would probably be accomplished by increasing both production capabilities and marketing efforts. The nonprofit venture would be an area where the organization has knowledge and experience. There is nothing fundamentally different in what it is trying to do. The nonprofit is just trying to do it better and to do more of it.

The second option is to sell an *existing* product or service to a *new* market. Perhaps the nonprofit has a very good service or product that could be useful to others. The organization believes it has saturated its current market, but there are opportunities in another market—an upscale market, a commercial clientele or a different location. This is a market expansion strategy. The organization would undertake an aggressive marketing campaign to sell the same product or service to a new group of people. The product or service would remain fundamentally unchanged. For our housing publication, the nonprofit may now try to sell the same magazine to real estate agents, banks, housing developers, real estate attorneys, government officials, urban planners, etc.

The third option capitalizes upon the *existing* relationships with clients, customers or vendors to sell a *new* product or service. The organization asks, "What would these people buy from us in addition to what they currently buy?" This is a product expansion strategy. Selling refreshments or T-shirts to the ballet audience or home health care to hospital patients are examples of product expansion strategies. The publishers of our housing journal may look at the housing advocacy groups who make up their current subscribers and develop a new line of products to sell them. These may include notebooks to hold the magazines, consulting services, a membership service package, a series of educational programs, video tapes, etc.

The fourth strategy is diversification. Diversification takes a *new* product into a *new* market. This is the riskiest of the four options. Diversification might involve our publisher in selling educational video tapes to corporate finance departments.

Market penetration is probably the least risky strategy, followed by market expansion, then product expansion and, finally, diversification.

By using the product development matrix, as well as the resource inventory and trend analysis, the nonprofit should be able to brainstorm 100 to 150 venture ideas. The ideas should represent possible matches between the organization, its skills and resources, and the environment in which it functions. Ideas should build on the nonprofit base, but not be limited by it. A dance company successfully runs a coffee house aided by a board member who used to manage such a business (diversification); a social service agency offers services to affluent seniors building on its knowledge and experience with low-income seniors (market expansion); a hospital offers management services to other hospitals based on its own management experience (market expansion); and a battered women's shelter successfully sells products mail-order to women (product expansion).

Next, the list is screened and refined until the nonprofit has a business idea with potential for a successful venture.

THE INITIAL SCREENING

The initial screening is based on knowledge within the nonprofit organization. It is a thoughtful "gut reaction" to the business ideas that have been generated through the brainstorming. The same people in the brainstorming group or another group of board and staff members can screen the business ideas. The collective knowledge of the group is used to make judgments about each of the 100 to 150 venture ideas—the appropriateness for the organization and the potential for market success.

The screening group will be surprised by the amount of knowledge it has about particular businesses. The group will be able to predict with a fair degree of accuracy the opportunities and shortcomings each idea presents. They will judge whether the opportunities are sufficient and the obstacles small enough to warrant further investigation. The primary criteria for initial selection is the extent to which an idea excites and would attract the organization to commit its resources, time and energy.

Without the enthusiasm and the support of the organization, the chances of any idea succeeding are few. A brilliant idea that does not have the support of the organization is doomed to failure. On the other hand, a less innovative idea has a stronger chance if the people within the organization are firmly committed to seeing it succeed.

Bankers and venture capitalists use two criteria in deciding to finance a business. Most important are the people and their commitment to the venture. The business idea is of secondary importance. A strong idea with a strong team will get first consideration, the weaker idea with a strong team will be considered second, and the strong idea with a weak team will probably get no support.

Deciding which business ideas to pursue further may seem arbitrary. From the list of 100 to 150 ideas, only four or five probably deserve further research. The resources available allow investigation of only four or five ideas. In addition, the nonprofit wants to avoid getting stuck in the research process, where research becomes an end in itself and the business venture never gets beyond the brainstorming phase.

The initial screening does not commit the organization to any of these ideas. Rather, these choices begin to narrow and define the ventures to be considered. As well, the choices lead the nonprofit to a better understanding of its own interests, its capabilities and its chances of success. The ultimate business concept may be very different from the initial idea considered, but it usually will have evolved from an idea selected from the initial screening.

OBJECTIVE CRITERIA

The research, planning and operation of a business is an evolutionary process. The successful entrepreneur is persistent, takes moderate risks and learns from his or her mistakes. In developing a business, the nonprofit must constantly re-evaluate and look at new approaches based on experience from the previous day. This learning process begins at this stage in the planning process when the nonprofit, for the first time, applies objective criteria to its business ideas. Openness and objectivity are crucial. Be prepared to let go of a favorite idea if it appears unrealistic under closer scrutiny.

All or some of the criteria described below may be used in screening business ideas. The first three criteria involve the organization's people resources and are the most important. Without very positive responses to these three, the business has little chance of moving forward, let alone succeeding. The appropriateness of the other criteria depends on the nature of the business venture.

- *Fit within the nonprofit corporation.* This broad criterion is probably the most important. To what extent is the business activity compatible with all aspects of the nonprofit organization? This does not mean that the venture must fit perfectly within current operations. But the venture cannot conflict with or undermine current operations. If the business can draw upon and advance current activities, this is an advantage. What is to be avoided is a business venture that will irreparably alienate clients, major funders, board members, staff or other key players within the nonprofit community. The business should be compatible with the values and politics of the nonprofit corporation. The nonprofit wants to avoid a business that would ignite strong negative reactions from the local business community, local politicians or other nonprofit corporations within the community. The business should not create unnecessary divisiveness or criticism. In addition, the nonprofit must evaluate the potential of the venture to meet the goals established by the organization.

- *Existence of a venture champion.* The champion is an individual relatively senior in the organization, on the staff or board, who has the time, energy and dedication to see the venture idea through. The champion will not necessarily manage the business, but he or she must be strongly committed to the business idea and must keep it moving ahead so that the idea proceeds through the planning process to a final decision and implementation. A business usually represents a diversion from the normal way the organization operates. A respected venture champion has the authority to keep the planning process moving and to harness the resources necessary to bring the idea to fruition. Without a champion, a business venture has little chance of success.

- *Management and staff capability to plan and start the venture.* Does the organization have in-house or can they secure the people and talent necessary to plan and initiate the venture? If the skills exist on staff, can they be freed up to work on the venture? If someone must be brought in from the outside, can the person be identified and are sufficient resources available to pay her/him? Should venture planning be added to existing responsibilities assigned to an individual or given to a venture team?

- *Proprietary character of product or service.* To what extent is the nonprofit capable of protecting the idea with copyrights or patents to assure a market advantage? Is the product in some way unique that will make it difficult for others to copy and steal your market?

- *Characteristics of the market.* Who will be the potential consumers? Where do they live? What are their buying patterns? Are these patterns consistent with the demographics of the community where you want to sell? Are these people you want to work with?

- *Entry barriers.* Barriers might include strong competition, high advertising budgets, union resistance, patents or required licenses that make it too expensive, difficult or impossible to break into a particular business.
- *Sales and profit potential.* Does the business have the potential to do sufficient sales to generate the kind of profits that you are interested in generating? A grocery store that generates one percent profits looks very different from a law office that may generate as much as 50 percent profit.
- *Investment.* How much money is needed to capitalize the business? Is it reasonable to expect this will be available?
- *Potential sources of capital.* Who might be interested in investing in this kind of business? Would these funds come from the organization's resources or from outside?
- *Downside risk.* If the business fails after full investment in its operation, what is the worst thing that could happen? Can the nonprofit survive that possibility?
- *Life of the product.* Will the product or service still be in demand ten or twenty years from now? Or will it have a short demand, after which the organization goes out of business? Ideally, a product or products would have a long life and a growing market.
- *Market trends within the industry.* Is this a market that is growing or declining?
- *Regulatory environment.* Are there federal, state or local rules related to the environment, to hiring, to location, to reporting or to licenses that should be considered before undertaking the venture?
- *Staff requirements.* What kind of staff is needed to operate the venture? This is a particularly important criterion if the organization is considering using clients to staff the business. Are people available with the needed skills to staff the business?
- *Availability of sites and location.* Is an appropriate site available for the venture? Is the organization located in the right geographic area for the kind of business planned?
- *Planning time required before start-up.* If the organization needs the business to be operational and generating income immediately, the choice of business may be very different from the organization that can wait three or four years before the business becomes operational or generates a positive cash flow.

This is not an exhaustive list of the criteria the organization might consider in evaluating its business ideas. The evaluation at this point is still very informal. The organization is looking for a few businesses in which there is sufficient interest and promise to merit further examination. Among the initial questions that must be answered is whether a particular business can accomplish the aims established in the goal-setting process described in the last chapter. These goals must remain in the foreground as a reminder of the reasons for starting a business and the results the business is meant to accomplish. A business that does not accomplish its goals, or move the organization closer to accomplishing its goals, fails to assist the nonprofit in achieving greater self-sufficiency and stabilization.

7 PRELIMINARY FEASIBILITY STUDIES

The preliminary feasibility study is the first research report to be prepared on the four or five selected business ideas. These are the ideas identified through the brainstorming process described in the previous chapter.

The preliminary feasibility study is a relatively brief summary written about each of the ideas selected on the basis of their compatibility with the organization and their perceived market potential. The study should be objective, not promotional, in tone. Its purpose is to identify all the elements and conditions that could prevent the business from succeeding. In this way, the nonprofit can eliminate the bad venture ideas and concentrate on the one or two remaining ideas that have the most potential. The organization can then devote greater research, time and resources to their development.

At the same time, the organization is gathering information about the business ideas to start shaping the venture into a more specific form. The preliminary feasibility study not only provides an overview of the business, its market and operation, but also raises many questions that must be answered before a go-ahead decision is made.

The questions raised by the preliminary feasibility study are valuable to consider in deciding whether a particular venture idea should proceed to the next step, which is preparing a full feasibility study. These questions become an important guide for the research conducted in the full feasibility study.

The preliminary feasibility study is still a part of the organization's screening process. It is a quick overview and runs from two to six or seven pages in length.

The preliminary feasibility study is a seven-step process. The first step is write down the venture goal. During the preliminary feasibility study process, the nonprofit organization will evaluate the venture for its poten-

FIGURE 7.1: Preliminary Feasibility Study Outline

I. State the venture goal.
II. Define the business.
III. Define the products or services of the business.
IV. Evaluate the description.
V. Conduct a market analysis.
VI. Conduct an operations and financial assessment.
VII. Evaluate the appropriateness and potential of the venture.

tial to achieve the venture goal, for its compatibility with the organization and for its market potential.

Steps two and three define the business and define the products the business sells. For example, a ballet company has a venture idea of selling food at performances. This is one of the venture ideas selected for conducting a preliminary feasibility study. At this point the idea could be selling candy before performances, subcontracting with McDonald's to run a fast-food operation in the theater, selling alcoholic beverages and snacks during intermission, opening a coffee and dessert bar to operate after performances, or serving catered dinners to patrons before performances.

The ballet company must define the business by deciding what they intend to sell, where they intend to sell it, when it will be sold, who it will be sold to, who will sell it, and how often. They need to decide if the food will include luxury or low-cost items, whether the service will be formal or informal, whether sales will be restricted to patrons or open to the public, what the hours of operation are to be, and so on.

You may wish to use the preliminary feasibility study to evaluate each of the options presented. This would essentially entail preparing six separate assessments—one for each idea.

In the third step, the ballet company defines the kinds of products involved in this business. The products include the services or items to be purchased by consumers. The business might sell desserts, coffee and sandwiches, or full-course meals. The business might sell alcoholic beverages or catering services. Hard products, such as decorated paper plates and napkins or other souvenir items, also might be sold to the patrons of the ballet company. The business might go so far as to offer consulting services to other performing arts companies interested in the same idea.

The more products that are sold, the more complicated the business becomes. Describing the business and describing its products helps to clarify and define the nonprofit's vision. The definition process in steps two and three help the organization to consider all the options available through the business venture. Through this process the business idea may evolve into something more exciting and with more potential for success than the original idea. Committing the definition of the business and its products to paper gives people a common ground on which to base further deliberations.

During step four, the nonprofit organization takes time to evaluate its description of the business. Is the group still comfortable with the idea? Is the group still committed to the venture? They may decide to abandon it at this point because it is no longer something they wish to pursue. Or they may find that the idea is exactly to their liking and that they are ready to do further research. A third option may be to revise the definition and come up with another version of the initial concept more to their liking.

If the venture idea merits further investigation, the nonprofit prepares a brief market analysis in step five of the preliminary feasibility study. This analysis examines factors necessary for the business to succeed by looking at the market environment for the business in question. A restaurant business is concerned primarily with local trends, while national trends and market conditions may be important to a software product. The nonprofit wants to identify, with as little work as possible, the trends within the market. Is it a growing or a declining market? What is the average sales level for this kind of business? What is the history of the industry under consideration? What are the characteristics of the market: who is the item sold to; how often is the product sold; and is there repeat business? What do similar businesses look like? What do they sell and how are their products or services priced? What are the characteristics, such as location, that lead to success or failure in this business?

The business analysis provides the most important information in the preliminary feasibility study. However, it is necessary to examine some of the operational and technical aspects of the business as well. In step six, the nonprofit determines whether it has the organizational capacity and capability to implement the business. What is involved in the production and merchandising process for this business? What kind of marketing is required and who does it? What kind of facilities, labor force and management are required? Are there prohibitive entry barriers? Understanding these requirements enables the organization to evaluate whether the skills and experience are available to operate the business.

In step six, the nonprofit also estimates its start-up capital requirements and, if appropriate, the time required for start-up operations. The nonprofit needs to obtain financial data on the profitability of the business. What is the average profit margin for this industry? What are the average gross sales? Do these numbers vary by region or by size of business? How long does it take to achieve these levels of sales and profitability?

In steps five and six, the nonprofit organization has prepared a brief business analysis and examined operational and technical aspects of the business. In step seven, the nonprofit evaluates the appropriateness and potential of the business venture. These questions are similar to those asked earlier, but they can now be answered on the basis of more data. Does the business fit with the nonprofit? Does the venture support the nonprofit's mission and its clients? Does the organization have the capacity to take on this venture? Does it have the potential to succeed in the marketplace? Does the idea still sound exciting?

A simplified list of items that should be examined to evaluate the potential feasibility of new businesses and acquisitions includes:

New Businesses
- what the business sells
- how the product is manufactured or purchased for resale
- the trade area
- current and potential market
- competition
- keys to business success
- sales potential
- labor skill required
- management skill required
- *capital* required
- net *profit* potential
- availability of financing
- failure risk

Business Acquisitions (in addition to those above):
- why the owner is selling
- current and past three year's income statements
- past three year's income tax returns
- current balance sheet
- current customer list

Other factors you may wish to consider in the preliminary assessment are:
- available management talent
- technical requirements

- direct competition with large industries
- nature of goods produced, such as style sensitive apparel
- availability of raw materials and goods purchased for resale

INFORMATION RESOURCES

Sources of information for preparing the preliminary feasibility study are many. The best information sources on most businesses are the national, and sometimes the local, trade associations. The trade associations for hundreds of industries and businesses are listed in the annual publication *National Trade and Professional Associations of the United States*, available in any reference library. Each of these organizations does research on its industry and will provide information to people interested or involved in the business. Industry journals and other publications, as well as inquiries to the staff of the trade association, can provide most of the information needed.

Trade associations may charge for reports or request membership in the association. But information that costs $50 or $75 may save hundreds of dollars in staff time spent researching or may save thousands of dollars by preventing the nonprofit from undertaking a lost-cause venture.

People experienced in the business are another source of information if they are not threatened by potential competition. They may be more open if they know that the venture is related to charitable activities. The nonprofit can talk with business people located sufficiently distant from its community, or with people in related businesses, such as suppliers or customers.

The president or chief executive officer of a business may be less forthcoming than a middle manager. The nonprofit may be able to obtain better information on how an industry operates from an experienced middle manager than from a more senior, more protective official. In any case, the organization should attempt to obtain the needed information from as few sources as possible.

The nonprofit organization should be alert for articles in magazines, newspapers and trade journals. Articles in the *Wall Street Journal* can be valuable sources of information, and financial institutions often prepare analyses of industries for investment purposes. These reports provide a great deal of background information on the economic health and trends of particular industries.

If you are in doubt about how to research a particular business, the reference librarian at your local business school or business library can help you identify and locate the best sources of information.

DECISION POINT

At any point in researching the preliminary feasibility study, the nonprofit may conclude that the business idea is not worthy of further consideration. When this becomes clear, it is time to stop researching that idea. Time is valuable and must not be wasted. The purpose of feasibility research is to eliminate bad ideas as quickly as possible, to retool ideas with potential and to identify the one or two ideas that may have a chance to succeed.

Each preliminary feasibility study should conclude with an evaluation of the strengths and weaknesses of each venture, and the four or five studies should be laid out side by side so that comparisons can be made. Usually, one idea will emerge as the clear winner. If none is attractive, go back to brainstorming and start again. If more than one idea emerges, rank them in order of preference. Unless you are a large and diverse organization, it is better to pursue one idea at a time. Get the first one established before starting another.

8 THE FULL FEASIBILITY STUDY

The next step in the organization's business development process is the full feasibility study. During the preliminary feasibility study phase, the nonprofit narrowed the number of business ideas under consideration to the one or two having the greatest market potential.

The organization now focuses on the single business idea that has attracted the greatest interest and appears to have the greatest potential. A full feasibility study should now be prepared on this business activity. Having a second business activity as a backup is often a good idea, in case the first proves to be unworkable. A fallback business idea often allows the organization to be more objective in evaluating the information collected.

The organization undertakes the feasibility study with two objectives: evaluating in detail the *potential* of the venture and its unique *requirements*. The nonprofit must be objective, even skeptical, in its research. Problems must be identified to see if they may be overcome. At the same time, the nonprofit is learning how to make the business venture work. Through learning about an industry, a market and the operation of a business, the nonprofit becomes better able to define and describe a business that either can or cannot succeed.

The end product of a feasibility study is a formal written document. The average report may be between fifty and sixty pages in length; size varies greatly with the complexity of the business. However, the purpose of the feasibility study is not just the product but also the educational process. The goal is to learn about the business, the market and the operation, not to design a specific business operation. By learning through the experiences of others, their successes and failures, the nonprofit can assess the potential of the business.

There are four parts to the full feasibility study: business definition, market analysis, operations overview and financial planning. Although much of the data for the four sections may be collected at the same time, there is an advantage to preparing the four parts in order. At the end of each part, the nonprofit has the opportunity to evaluate the information collected and analyzed to that point and to decide if the business idea is unfeasible. Rather than completing the study, the organization might abandon the particular venture idea or redefine the idea and begin the research process anew. There is also an opportunity at the end of each section to evaluate what additional questions must be researched. The feasibility study is a working document to be used in preparing the business plan, and financing and managing the business. A good feasibility study will reduce the amount of risk in starting a new business.

BUSINESS DEFINITION

The business definition part of the full feasibility study has six steps. The first, as in the preliminary feasibility study, is to write down the goals of the venture: what should the venture accomplish for the nonprofit? how much income should the venture generate? how many people should it employ? how much start-up capital should be required? etc. At the end of each major part of the feasibility study, the nonprofit will evaluate the business against this goal statement. If the business does not meet these goals, the nonprofit should seriously reconsider the venture.

The second step, to define the business, and third step, to define the products, are discussed in greater detail in Chapter Seven, Preliminary Feasibility Studies and are not repeated here. The business and product definitions may have changed as a result of the preliminary research, and those changes should be incorporated into the full feasibility study. The business and product definitions spell out the venture concept, and are a basis for testing and further research.

The fourth step is to test the concept. Before further research or committing additional resources, the nonprofit wants to know if potential consumers like the business idea, whether they have any suggestions for improvement and whether they would buy the product or service. In testing the business idea, the organization wants feedback from potential consumers about price, design, distribution, frequency of use by the target consumer population, alternative uses and other consumer reactions. Testing is a critical point in the research process. Through testing consumers' reactions, the nonprofit discovers whether its product or service has any appeal in the marketplace.

The nonprofit organization should be sure to test its business idea with the appropriate consumer. A product designed for children should appeal to children, but the purchasing decision will be made by parents or other adults. Gift items designed for executives may be purchased by spouses, secretaries or purchasing agents, not by business executives. In small corporations, the chief executive officer may influence purchasing

FIGURE 8.1: The Feasibility Study Outline

Part I: Business Definition
1. State venture goals.
2. Define the business.
3. Define the products.
4. Test the business idea.
5. Refine the idea.
6. Evaluate the business.

Part II: Market Analysis
7. Research the market.
8. Identify competitors.
9. Specify competitive advantages.
10. Estimate market share.
11. Identify marketing and sales strategies.
12. Evaluate the business.

Part III: Operations Overview
13. Outline the production or merchandising process.
14. Profile the labor force.
15. Determine management staff requirements.
16. Evaluate the business.

Part IV: Financial Planning
17. Prepare pro forma start-up budget.
18. Prepare pro forma income statement.
19. Prepare pro forma cash flow analysis.
20. Evaluate the business.

---

decisions, but in large corporations, decisions are made by a purchasing agent or purchasing department. The nonprofit must discover through its own thinking and some investigation who will be the purchaser of its product or service.

There are a variety of ways to test the business idea. The nonprofit could distribute a survey to a number of people. The survey might include a drawing of the product or description of the service and would ask people to respond to questions about the product or service. The survey results would be tabulated and evaluated.

The nonprofit could convene a focus group of seven to twelve potential consumers to discuss their habits and preferences related to the product or service. Of interest are their current needs and behaviors, as well as their reactions to the particular product or service idea.

Product testing can be supplemented by interviews about the product idea with people knowledgeable about a particular industry, location or population. For example, a buyer for a department store understands what does and does not sell in a particular market.

The nonprofit could develop a sample product, or prototype, and ask people to react to it. In comparative testing, as has been done with cola drinks, people are asked about their preferences, and sometimes are asked to make pre-production commitments. For example, a housing construction organization ran a newspaper advertisement asking people interested in a particular kind of housing to attend a meeting. At the meeting, they were asked to sign a pledge that if the housing were built, they wanted to be first to have the opportunity to buy. Attendance at the meeting and willingness to sign the pledge indicated market interest for the housing product.

A small pilot operation is sometimes an informative means of testing a product or service idea. One organization was interested in starting a catering business. Before undertaking a full-scale operation they decided to test the idea by catering on a small scale during the December holidays. They discovered there was market interest in their catering services, and they received considerable external support for the business, but they found it was impossible internally for them to operate such a business. They abandoned the idea based on internal rather than external market considerations.

Testing the business idea provides information to understand the market and market choices and to understand what is needed to operate the business successfully. It is helpful to get advice from marketing experts to design and evaluate concept tests.

The fifth step is to revise the definitions of the business and the product, based on the feedback obtained through testing. The new definitions are then tested to see if the revised product or service elicits the desired market acceptance. This process may lead the nonprofit away from its original idea or it may simply sharpen the original business concept.

In the sixth step, the nonprofit takes time to evaluate the evolved business idea. How does the business as now defined fit with the organization? Will the business still have the support of the board and the staff? Will the business alienate important constituencies? Will the business achieve the established goals? This step is a checkpoint, the first of four evaluation decisions in the feasibility study process. If the business is no longer right for the organization, or has no market acceptance, it is time to abandon it and investigate another venture idea.

MARKET ANALYSIS

In this part of the feasibility study, the nonprofit organization fully researches the size, trends and characteristics of the market, and identifies and evaluates its competition. The organization is then able to estimate its market share, to explore marketing and sales techniques, and to evaluate if there is a promising market niche.

Market analysis takes place before considering operations or financing. Understanding the market, particularly for a new business, is a critical factor in business success. Although poor management and underfinancing are major contributors to business failure, many business people—individuals, private corporations and nonprofit organizations—cite inadequate understanding of the market or overestimating the market as the major cause of business failure. In addition, the market research provides insight into the factors contributing to success or failure in a particular industry.

The seventh step of the full feasibility study is to research the market. The nonprofit should identify the major market trends and the significant factors influencing the market. The trends and influences should be examined first on a national level, then on a local level. The market research includes not only the trends of the industry and factors influencing it, but also the trends and other factors influencing consumers of the particular product or service.

The examination of the industry should cover the following: its size; its rate of growth or decline; the different segments of the industry and their growth rates; recent diversification or consolidation trends; projections; the markets in which the industry operates; distribution techniques used in the industry; relationships with foreign labor or foreign markets; effects of existing or proposed legislation; pricing; product trends; technological trends; and anticipated changes, problems or opportunities.

The research should include a demographic profile of the consumers, where they live, their sex, age and educational level. How much, on average, do the consumers spend for the product or service in question? How often do they buy? What factors influence their purchasing decisions? Are the consumers changing in number or in their characteristics? Are new consumers targeted for future products?

Geographic concentration of the industry and the consumer population also should be examined. Are they located in urban, suburban or rural areas? Does it seem to make any difference? Is there a need to be located at the intersection of or near a major highway? Are there critical geographic ratios affecting the success of the business, such as distance to the nearest competitor, average travel time or concentration of population?

National market data is examined first, for two reasons. First, data aggregated on a national level is more likely to be available. Second, the trends and influencing factors revealed in the national data can then be compared to local conditions.

Assume, for example, that the national data identify the following factors as critical to the successful operation of a senior citizens retirement center: the number of senior citizens falling within a certain income bracket; the number of senior citizens of a certain religious or ethnic background; and the number of senior citizens living within easy traveling distance. Transportation routes, parking or other factors may be important. The interested nonprofit organization can then look at local census data within its community to see if local reality matches the conditions identified as critical to success.

The sources for this kind of information are the same as those recommended for the preliminary feasibility studies. National and state business trade associations are major sources, as are the U.S. Census Bureau and Commerce Department. In addition to the population census, the federal government conducts a business census and agricultural census every seven years. The U.S. Commerce Department collects information on economic development within certain industries, as do small business development centers. Business trade journals and investment houses provide information from slightly different perspectives. People working within an industry, such as strategic planners, business owners and operators, often provide more information than can be gained from any other source.

The eighth step in the full feasibility study is to identify competitors within the specified local market. The nonprofit should identify competitors and find out as much as possible about them. Through researching the competition, the nonprofit will learn who is succeeding and who is struggling, and how they are operating. This research may uncover an untapped marked niche or a means to capture market shares from the competition.

First, the nonprofit should make a list of the names and addresses of all its potential competitors. Sources for the list include: the yellow pages of the telephone book; listings compiled by the federal or state commerce departments and by Dun & Bradstreet; trade associations and the Chamber of Commerce; and talking with competitors, their suppliers and customers.

Next, the nonprofit needs to discover certain details about the operations of each competitor. These details include: number of employees; annual sales level; number of years in business; number of years before achieving profitability; the products they currently sell and those they plan to introduce; their target consumers; the geographic area they serve; their key suppliers; their distribution techniques; their marketing and sales techniques; the contract terms they offer; their payment schedule; the unique qualities of their products or services; and how they differentiate themselves from other businesses in the industry.

Some of this information can be obtained from secondary sources, such as news articles, annual reports or sales and promotional materials. Other information can be collected by observing the company. The best source is a face-to-face interview with someone within the competing corporation. Interview access might be achieved by playing the role of a customer, researcher or student.

Only by knowing and understanding the competition can the nonprofit business venture separate itself from the competition, or gain an advantage by identifying an untapped market. There are only two types of customers: people who have never before bought the product or service and current customers of the competition. In either case, the nonprofit must present a compelling reason for the consumer to purchase its product or service.

The ninth step of the full feasibility study is to specify the competitive advantage of the nonprofit's service or product. By comparing the nonprofit's tested business design with the competition, the organization can distinguish its business from the competitor's. The nonprofit's competitive advantage in the marketplace is substantiated by data from its earlier tests. Competitive advantages often involve price, location, distribution technique or product differentiation. The advantage over the competition must be clearly and objectively specified because it becomes the focus of the organization's efforts in marketing and operating the business.

Informed about the characteristics of the market, the competition and its own competitive advantage, the nonprofit proceeds to estimate its market share, the tenth step in preparing the full feasibility study. The estimated market share is expressed in terms of the projected number of customers, and in the dollar value of their projected purchases. The tendency to overestimate should be kept in mind when preparing these projections.

Market share is estimated based on the following factors: the behavior and relative success of competitors; the resources to be invested in the business; the base from which the nonprofit operates; the nonprofit's current links to the market and the industry; the nonprofit's competitive advantage; its production capability; and the trends within the industry. The projection is based on these factors within an overall context of the size and growth of the market.

It is recommended that the nonprofit project a range for its estimated market share (from a worst possible case to a best possible case) and then cut both ends of the range in half to compensate for overestimation. With the market share projection the nonprofit can calculate the potential income of the business. Would the profit from the estimated market share satisfy the goals set for the venture? It is not necessary for the nonprofit to corner a substantial share of the market, only a market share sufficient to operate the business as envisioned.

Step eleven of the full feasibility study is to identify the marketing and sales strategies. The nonprofit must determine what is necessary to market and sell the product in order to achieve the estimated market share. The organization should research marketing techniques, sales techniques, contract terms, marketing strategy, staffing for marketing and sales, the ways to convey the desired marketing image, advertising and promotion techniques and methods for closing deals. During the feasibility study, the organization should evaluate the effectiveness of several different marketing strategies and sales techniques. In this way, the nonprofit can choose the best approach to include in its business plan.

Step twelve is another opportunity to evaluate the business venture. Once again, the nonprofit should question the venture's fit with the organization. In addition, the nonprofit should ask: Is the market sufficient to achieve the venture goals? Are there marketing and sales techniques appropriate to the organization and effective in this market? Does the organization have a realistic competitive advantage? And does the competitive advantage translate into a sufficient share of the market? If the market is insufficient, is it better to abandon the business concept at this time than to pursue a business venture that cannot succeed?

OPERATIONS OVERVIEW

The third part of the full feasibility study provides an overview of what is involved in operating the business venture under consideration. Up to this point the research has focused on external factors affecting the business. Now the feasibility study concentrates on the day-to-day operational requirements of a successful business.

In this section of the feasibility study, the nonprofit's venture concept begins to assume more of the trappings of reality. This is helpful not only to determine the elements necessary to success, but also to judge how the business operation will mesh with the existing nonprofit operation. There may be existing resources and relationships that could serve both the new venture and the parent nonprofit.

The operations overview is not an operating plan, but an overview of operating requirements. An operating plan is sometimes prepared as part of the business plan or in a separate operations manual. Step thirteen in preparing the full feasibility plan is to outline the production or merchandising process.

The step-by-step outline describes each stage of the operation and the requirements of each stage. How do supplies and materials move through the process? What kind of equipment and supplies are required? How often must supplies be ordered and under what terms? Where do they come from? Is there a particular floor layout or location required? What are the storage, packaging and shipping requirements? Are spoilage, handling or inventory control special problems, and how might they be solved? What about theft and cash handling? How are orders taken and managed?

As in all parts of the feasibility study, the information included depends on the nature of the business. Whether the nonprofit plans to pursue a manufacturing, distribution or service business, there is a sequence of events that takes place. Understanding the steps, time intervals and requirements in the sequence assists in estimating the cost of goods sold, start-up costs, staffing requirements and management headaches.

Step fourteen is to develop a profile of the labor force in this business. The labor force profile should include: number required at various stages of operation; methods of recruitment; skills and special training; salaries, benefits and salary increments; employment terms and conditions, such as union contracts; average turnover; supervision requirements; and any other characteristics peculiar or beneficial to this business.

Step fifteen is to determine the managerial, administrative and sales staff requirements of the business. The nonprofit should collect information similar to that collected for the labor force profile. What kinds of skills and training and experience are required of the business manager? What other positions with what requirements are needed to staff the venture? Should specialists work full time or on a consulting basis? Should operations and marketing be separate from overall management? How many people need to be hired, how should they be compensated, and should performance contracts be considered? What salary levels and benefits are standard in the industry?

Research should cover the skills necessary to operate the business and the best ways to identify, attract and compensate skilled staff. A competent management team is essential to business success, whether its members are drawn from within the nonprofit or recruited from outside the organization. By establishing the job specifications first, the nonprofit can evaluate candidates objectively.

Step sixteen of the feasibility study is a third opportunity to evaluate the business venture. This evaluation is conducted with the benefit of greater understanding of the production or merchandising process, and of the people needed to perform and oversee the steps in the process. Are the steps in the production or merchandising process, and the types of employees required by the business, compatible with the nonprofit organization? Are there potential problems in supplies, distribution or storage? Is a suitable and sufficient labor force available or trainable? If the nonprofit plans to employ its clients, do the requirements of the labor force match the capabilities of the client population? Can the nonprofit attract and compensate qualified management staff? Is the organization comfortable with the overall requirements of the business?

FINANCIAL PLANNING

In the fourth and final part of the full feasibility study, the nonprofit prepares pro forma or projected financial statements based on the research collected in the market analysis and the operations overview. Steps seventeen, eighteen and nineteen are to prepare a pro forma start-up budget, income statement and cash flow analysis. These financial statements and their use as planning tools are described in detail in Chapter Eleven.

Step twenty, to evaluate the venture for a fourth time based primarily on the financial characteristics of the business, completes the full feasibility study.

The completed feasibility study should be reviewed by an expert to protect against overlooking critical factors, interpreting data preferentially, or reaching invalid conclusions. The objectivity of the study is critical to the organization's credibility in presenting the business venture to its board, its clients, its donors and prospective financiers. In addition, the study provides the knowledge necessary to make informed decisions about the business. A feasibility study cannot guarantee business success, but the educational process and the multiple evaluation checkpoints built into preparation of the full feasibility study can reduce the chances of a failure.

9 EVALUATING THE TAX CONSEQUENCES OF EARNING MONEY

*E*xamination of the tax consequences of earning money begins with a brief overview of the legal structure of the nonprofit organization. A nonprofit agency is a legal corporation organized most often under the laws of the state in which it operates. Nonprofit corporations differ fundamentally from other corporations in the state in that they are created to provide a public good. The definition of what constitutes a public good is written into the corporate law under which the nonprofit organizes. Typically, the public good includes education, religion, culture, research and assistance to the needy.

The charter or certificate of incorporation that the nonprofit submits to the Secretary of State for approval must state the service it will perform to benefit the public. In order to maintain its status, the nonprofit must operate in a manner consistent with its stated mission and designation as a nonprofit corporation.

Nonprofit corporations are technically owned by the citizens of the state in which they are incorporated. The nonprofit organization operates on their behalf and for their benefit. Unlike a business corporation, the nonprofit corporation does not have stockholders who receive benefits; rather, the nonprofit corporation must operate to benefit all the people of the state. Nonprofits cannot distribute assets or dividends to benefit individuals or members of its board of trustees. The Secretary of State designates the nonprofit's board of trustees to represent the people of the state and to hold the organization's assets in trust, and the board must manage the assets in keeping with the mission of the corporation. Upon dissolution of a nonprofit corporation, the assets are either returned to the state for redistribution or are distributed to another nonprofit corporation. In either case, the assets remain in the public domain and do not benefit any individuals.

Tax-exempt status is conferred by the IRS upon petition by the nonprofit corporation. Nonprofits designated as 501(c)(3) corporations are generally exempted from income tax, and contributions made to the nonprofit are deductible by the donor. The information that follows applies most specifically to nonprofits designated as 501(c)(3) organizations.

Although the legal structure of the nonprofit corporation differs from the business corporation, the activities it may undertake are substantially the same. Both may enter into contracts, may invest, borrow or lend money and may buy or sell products or services.

The payment of taxes is another important difference between the business corporation and the nonprofit corporation. The business corporation always pays income taxes on its net income; that is, income after expenses. Most nonprofits pay no income tax. However, in some situations nonprofits pay income tax, particularly when their operation closely resembles that of a business corporation. In some cases, if the nonprofit operation too closely resembles a business corporation, the nonprofit corporation may lose its tax-exempt status.

The most important reason to examine the tax consequences of earning money is that it is possible for a nonprofit to lose its federal tax-exempt status for improper reporting and payment of taxes. In addition, a tax obligation is a corporate liability. Back tax payments and fines can seriously undermine the financial standing of the organization, and board members may be held personally liable.

Finally, understanding the tax consequences of a business venture may influence an organization's selection of the product or service it will sell to raise funds. This chapter focuses exclusively on the federal income tax. Each nonprofit will have to examine the consequences on other taxes. Most states require the nonprofit corporation to pay sales tax on items sold by the organization, and there is a growing trend among local jurisdictions to require nonprofits to pay real estate taxes. Often, the activity taking place on the property weighs heavily in the decision to grant an exemption from property taxes. Real estate taxes can impose an unexpected burden on the budget of the nonprofit organization. Understanding tax implications is important in planning a business venture.

The balance of this chapter provides a basic guide to the current federal law affecting nonprofit corporations. Hearings held in 1987 reviewed some of the subjects covered in this chapter and changes in the nonprofit tax law seem likely. In any tax matter, the organization should check with its attorney. Planning a business venture should not be based solely on the information presented here.

THE INTERNAL REVENUE SERVICE

It is important to understand a few basics about the Internal Revenue Service (IRS) and how it operates. The mission of the IRS is to collect taxes owed the federal government as defined by existing law. The mission is straightforward, leaving little room for interpretation. The interpretation comes into play in analyzing the application of the law.

EVALUATING THE TAX CONSEQUENCES OF EARNING MONEY

Since tax law is relatively vague, a great deal of discretion is left to the agents of the IRS. When challenged, the discretion exercised by the IRS is ruled upon by the federal court system or the U.S. Tax Court. The IRS clearly warns that there is no precedent set by any rulings. A ruling made in California does not set precedent for a similar situation in New Jersey. Each case is decided on the facts and circumstances of that particular case and the application of the law as seen by the judge or IRS agent who reviews the case. IRS rulings and court rulings can provide insight into trends, but cannot provide concrete answers regarding what is or is not permissible.

The IRS operates under the fundamental assumption that every individual and every corporation, whether it is nonprofit or not, must pay taxes unless the contrary can be proved to the IRS. When a nonprofit corporation files its Form 990, it is saying to the IRS, "We are continuing in the activity for which we were granted tax-exempt status. If challenged, we must provide the information proving that the exemption should stand." The burden of proof is always on the taxpayer, not on the IRS. It is up to the nonprofit organization to maintain the records that build the case that exempt payments of taxes on income received.

BASIC SOURCES OF INCOME

Under certain circumstances, nonprofits are required to pay taxes on income received by the corporation. This determination is based primarily on the source of the income, not on the use to which the funds are allocated. Nonprofits receive the majority of their income from four basic sources:

The first income source is gifts and donations. Donors give money or other items to the nonprofit corporation and receive nothing in return except satisfaction and a deduction on their income tax. There are no considerations and no restrictions on the use of the funds, unless a specific use of the funds has been mutually agreed upon.

Grants are the second source of income. The nonprofit provides no special consideration to the grantor. Usually the money is given for a specific purpose and a legal contract ties the use of the funds to that purpose.

A third source of nonprofit income is business activity. Business activity may or may not be related to the purpose of the organization. The nonprofit is engaged in providing a service or product in exchange for financial or other consideration. Examples of nonprofit business activities include operating a gift shop, selling publications and charging fees for counseling services.

The fourth source of nonprofit income is passive income, such as rents, royalties, interest and dividends.

The IRS examines sources of income to determine whether they are related or unrelated to the organization's mission. Does the income-generating activity advance the mission of the nonprofit corporation other than by providing a source of income? The income-generating activity is considered unrelated if it does not directly further the nonprofit's mission.

For example, a nonprofit health education program decides to sell Swiss Army knives. It plans to earn a substantial amount of money through the sale of knives and to use the profits to provide free clinic services to potential AIDS victims. The income from the sale of the knives is clearly unrelated. Although the income would be used to advance the corporation's health mission, the exchange of money for a Swiss Army knife is unrelated to health education. Were the same health education agency to sell AIDS test kits or to charge fees for its counseling clinics, the income-generating activity would advance the health education mission, and the funds would be related income.

A nonprofit corporation with a source of related income may charge as much as it wants for the product or service, and can earn substantial profits without paying taxes on that income. However, unrelated income must be reported to the IRS on Form 990T, and taxes must be paid on net income in excess of one thousand dollars at the effective corporate tax rate. Failure to report unrelated income and pay taxes can result in penalties and fines. A nonprofit that generates too much unrelated income may lose its tax-exempt status.

How much is too much unrelated income is subject to interpretation. The formula commonly used to assess unrelated income is the ratio of gross unrelated income to total gross income. If the ratio approaches 15 to 20 percent, the nonprofit corporation may want to limit or eliminate sources of unrelated income. The 15 to 20 percent figure is based on an examination of case law and IRS rulings as well as on the advice of several tax attorneys. Some people believe the ratio can be as high as 25 percent. Conservative trends and the need for the IRS to collect greater revenues would argue that the 25 percent figure is too high.

Review of the four basic sources of nonprofit income eliminates some sources from tax consideration. Donation and gifts are always related to the nonprofit corporation. Money or other items are donated for the express purpose of furthering the mission of the corporation with no consideration given to the donor. In almost all cases, grants to the nonprofit corporation are related income. Funds are given to the corporation for a specific purpose related to the organization's mission.

Passive income is generally related income. Some exceptions to this rule will be discussed later in this chapter. The income generated through business activity may be either related or unrelated. The source of most unrelated income is from business activity. There are several rules which we will examine which help to determine whether the funds generated from passive income of business activity are related or unrelated income.

TESTS FOR RELATED AND UNRELATED INCOME

The terms *related* and *unrelated* refer to the mission of the nonprofit organization. The IRS defines the mission by two primary tests—the organizational test and the operational test.

The organizational test is the basic definition of the corporation. The IRS examines the charter of the corporation, the basis on which the original tax-exempt status was granted. The charter includes phrases that define a charitable, religious, educational or other valid nonprofit purpose as the exclusive activity of the corporation. The nonprofit corporation agrees that it will engage exclusively in this activity in order to maintain its tax-exempt status.

In the operational test, the IRS examines operating records and documents, such as audits, annual reports, evaluation reports and grant applications, to determine what the organization has been doing since its date of incorporation. These records refine the usually broad definition included in the charter, and reveal the extent to which the activities are in keeping with the charitable purpose for which the nonprofit was chartered.

When the nonprofit's activities are no longer *primarily* supportive of the mission for which it was created, the tax-exempt status of the corporation is threatened. The ratio of unrelated income to total income raises this issue because, by definition, unrelated income is not generated by activity that advances the mission of the organization.

The nonprofit organization should apply the same tests as does the IRS: it should look at its charter to see what it should be doing, and it should look at its records to see how it has been engaged. It may be beneficial or necessary to update the organization's charter to reflect current activities before any new activities are added. The organization may want to broaden its charter to incorporate any future activities contemplated.

The nonprofit organization is generating unrelated sales income if answers to all three of the following questions are affirmative. If the answer to any one of the three questions is negative, the income is related and therefore, non-taxable. These three questions constitute the basic test for unrelated sales income.

(1) Is the organization engaged in a trade or business? If the organization is engaged in an activity where a service or a product is exchanged for a cash or non-cash consideration, the answer is yes. (If there is no business

transaction, the organization is engaged in a related activity and does not have to answer questions two and three.)

(2) Is the business activity conducted on a regular basis? The question is whether the business activity is carried on with the frequency and continuity of a similar commercial venture.

An example may be helpful to understand the question. A nonprofit corporation runs an annual dinner dance. Money is paid to attend a banquet where food is served and entertainment is provided. The donor of the funds is the beneficiary and a direct exchange takes place. This is clearly a business activity for the nonprofit, even if the food, room and music have been donated. Is this activity conducted on a regular basis? An annual event is a regular event, but is very different from a commercial night club or dinner club operating a similar type of business. The frequency and continuity of the dinner dance is not carried out in a commercial manner. The answer to the second question is no. However, the answer would be yes if a dinner dance were held every Saturday night. If the business activity is intermittent, the income earned from the activity is related. The concept of *regularly carried on* must consider not only the event itself but the planning and follow-up time involved. A one-day event may take 374 days to plan. This may now constitute a regularly carried on activity

(3) Does the business activity contribute substantially to accomplishing the nonprofit's mission? If the activity does not contribute substantially, the income is unrelated. However, if the activity contributes substantially to the nonprofit's mission, the income is related. The significance of the activity, its scope and the disposition of the product must be measured in terms of importance to each organization's mission. A product defined as related to one organization may be unrelated to another, since charters and missions differ. Each situation must be examined individually.

Usually activities conducted as part of a training program, such as an auto body shop run by a vocational program or dance performances regularly scheduled by a ballet school, contribute significantly to an organization's mission. The training program has an instructor, a course curriculum and a schedule for completion, and participation in the income-generating activity is a reasonable requirement for graduation.

Services provided for the convenience of clients or members can contribute significantly to an organization's mission. Services provided to university students, such as dormitories, laundry service and the book store, are necessary for students to participate in the educational activities of the institution. Similarly, a restaurant within a museum and a cafeteria for hospital staff are services necessary to the organization's members, and therefore, they are related to the organization's mission.

Educational products and services can be related to a nonprofit's mission. These include books, art reproductions, manuals, educational toys and the like. Business activities that are, in fact, the service provided by the organization—tuition to a university, tickets sold by a performing arts organization or fees charged for counseling sessions by a social service agency to its regular clientele, of course, contribute significantly to the organization's mission.

There is an additional exemption specified in the tax code for any nonprofit sales activity where substantially all labor is volunteered or all goods sold are donated. A thrift shop selling donated goods, operated by volunteer or paid labor would be a related sales activity. The sale of T-shirts and mugs by volunteers during intermission at a ballet performance would be a related sales activity. Either the goods must be donated or the labor volunteered. A nonprofit consignment shop run by paid labor, where the donor is paid some amount for the goods, would not be an allowable activity under this exemption.

Question three raises the issue of whether the business activity comes within the scope of the nonprofit organization. Does the business activity meet the organizational and operational tests described earlier in this chapter? Is the business activity within the geographic limit, activity limit, client limit or other limits established by the charter? For example, if a counseling program established to serve underprivileged youth opened a clinic to serve more privileged clients, this could create a scope problem with unrelated income as a result. A program chartered to operate solely within New York State that provides substantial services in New Jersey may also have a scope problem.

A third type of scope problem arises when a nonprofit agency does more than is necessary to accomplish its mission. The auto body repair shop run by the vocational school provides an example. In the industry, standard training time on auto body repair requires, say, four months. But the nonprofit vocational school is running a successful, income-generating auto body repair shop and extends the training period to one year. In this case, the nonprofit has four months of related activity and eight months of unrelated activity. The nonprofit is doing more than is necessary, according to industry standards, to accomplish its mission.

The third issue raised by question three is the disposition of the product. This means that the product must be sold in substantially the same form it is in when the nonprofit completes its activity. For example, a workshop for the blind that produces rough wooden toys may not take these toys to be polished, painted and shellacked before they are sold. The product is altered substantially. There can be a mix of handicapped and nonhandicapped workers or some professional assistance, in which case the recommended ratio is 25 percent of the work performed by non-handicapped and 75 percent by the handicapped workers. Wholesaling the products to a finisher would be allowable, however, since they are finally sold by the nonprofit in substantially the same shape.

The nonprofit organization generates unrelated income if it answers the three questions affirmatively: is the organization engaged in a trade or business? is the business activity conducted on a regular basis? and does the business activity not contribute substantially to accomplishing the nonprofit's mission? There is nothing wrong with unrelated income as long as it is reported, taxes are paid and it is not too much.

The recent challenges to nonprofit organizations, as reported by the U.S. Small Business Administration, have focused on these three issues in determining whether income is related or unrelated and should be taxable. Many challenges have claimed that the business activities run by nonprofits do not relate to accomplishing their mission; others claim that captive markets and subsidies make competition "unfair." There is room for interpretation.

Many YMCAs today operate health clubs for professionals and business executives. Commercial health spa owners have charged these programs are unrelated to the YMCA mission. The focus has been on the fee structure and the client population. The challengers have claimed that these are not the clients the YMCA was established to serve, and that the fee structure prohibits the availability of services to the traditional client population.

Similarly, hospitals have been charged as being non-charitable institutions because they do not serve a large enough proportion of indigent patients. Other nonprofit business activities, such as day-care, hearing aid sales, travel services, testing laboratories and computer sales by educational institutions also have come under attack in recent years. These issues are being examined by Congress. Only the future will tell how the definition of related or unrelated nonprofit business activity may change.

The experience to date has been mixed. Some nonprofits have had their tax-exempt status upheld through the courts, while others have had portions of their activities ruled taxable. However, understanding the ways the IRS examines these issues and the criteria it uses to make an evaluation helps the nonprofit to decide whether a particular business activity would generate related or unrelated income.

It is important for a nonprofit organization to consider its sources of passive income. Passive income includes rent, royalties, interest and dividends. Consultation with a lawyer is advised when any of these matters is complicated.

If a nonprofit owns a building outright with no mortgage held by another institution or individual, the nonprofit can lease its property to anyone it chooses and the lease income is related income. This is true if the lease covers primarily real property, land and buildings. If, however, a majority of the property leased is personal property, such as furniture, equipment or services, the income may be taxable. The mix of personal and real property leased must be evaluated.

If the nonprofit property is mortgaged, the rental income is unrelated to the extent of the mortgage. For example, lease payments on a $1 million building with a $500,000 mortgage generate 50 percent related income and 50 percent unrelated income. If the nonprofit leases to tenants having missions similar to its own, the nonprofit is advancing its own mission and the income is related.

Using borrowed money to invest applies to real property and other investments. Dividends earned from stock purchases are unrelated income to the degree that a purchase was made with borrowed money. The interest earned on loaned money is taxable to the extent that the money was loaned from someone else. Interest earned on an investment is unrelated, and therefore taxable, to the extent the funds were borrowed from elsewhere.

TOO MUCH UNRELATED INCOME

If a nonprofit organization has unrelated income that is 15 percent or more of its total income, the organization has several options:

- *Revise the charter of the organization.* Depending on the nature of the business, the nonprofit can file papers with the IRS to amend its charter to include the unrelated activity in which it is involved. This should be done before the activity is undertaken. If this is a minor change or updating of the charter, there should be no problem. However, submitting a revised charter does expose the nonprofit to IRS scrutiny. This may be a lengthy process that could challenge the purpose of the entire organization.
- *Alter the business to make it related.* This option is not recommended. This is not the time to make hasty organizational changes, after the business has finally become successful.
- *Stabilize or reduce the income to below 15 percent.* This would be bad for the business and for the nonprofit. The goal is to generate as much money as possible to support the nonprofit and limiting income is bad for business.
- *Sell the business.* The nonprofit would have to evaluate whether the income from selling the business would be re-

lated income. If unrelated income, taxes would have to be paid on the sale. The nonprofit would have to consider whether the sale of the business would eliminate a potentially larger source of income to the organization.

- *Establish another nonprofit organization in which the business activity is related.* A cooperative partnership can be established under which the second nonprofit donates its profits from income generating activity to the parent nonprofit. An example of this relationship exists between the Metropolitan Opera and the Metropolitan Opera Guild. The two are nonprofit organizations with interlinking boards. The charter of the Opera Guild supports the arts with income earned through the sale of memberships and a wide variety of products. The Guild turns over its substantial profits to the Metropolitan Opera at the end of every year.

- *Establish a separate profit-making corporation.* There are several advantages to running the business activity as a separate corporation. As the sole owner of the corporation, the nonprofit is entitled to receive dividends from the corporation. In addition, stockholders exercise major control through the legal structure of the business corporation. They elect the board of directors and approve major policies. On a more operational level, the separate corporation provides clear direction and separates the unrelated business activity from the nonprofit. Each can be managed to its own purposes. Operations policies may vary for hiring and compensation of staff, employee benefits, unionization, marketing strategy, location, image, bookkeeping and financing. The relationship between the profit-making and the nonprofit corporations can be linked through overlapping membership on the boards. One board may not discuss or set policy that affects the other. However, interlocking boards provide knowledge and continuity that allow appropriate mutual support. The transfer of funds from the business corporation to the nonprofit take place in several forms. The primary means is through the distribution of dividends at the end of the corporate year. In addition, the business corporation is allowed to contribute up to 10 percent of before-tax profits to a nonprofit charity. The business corporation may also contract with the nonprofit for a variety of services, including bookkeeping, space and training. The contracts must be prepared in written form and establish a fair market value for the services, in order to avoid conflict of interest and charges of self-dealing. Some of this income may be unrelated. Careful structuring of the separate business corporation offers many benefits to the nonprofit, including liability protection and nullifying charges of unfair competition. This option requires additional bookkeeping and preparation of tax forms.

The nonprofit organization should weigh the advantages and disadvantages of the options before taking action, to protect itself from excessive unrelated income.

The primary concern in evaluating the tax consequences of earning money is to make sure the nonprofit has sufficient control of the business activity to prevent any tax problems. The business should serve the nonprofit, not destroy it.

Any business activity must be nurtured to provide as much income as possible to the nonprofit operation. The unrelated business activity must also be documented for tax purposes. The nonprofit must account for income and expenses, file separate IRS forms, and pay taxes on amounts in excess of $1,000.

The nonprofit organization must monitor the ratio of unrelated income to total income and be ready to take action if the business activity threatens the well-being of the organization.

Whether a business venture is related or unrelated to the organization's mission is among the factors the nonprofit should consider in selecting a business idea. Some nonprofits place a high value on this criteria; others see the issue as relatively minor.

Related and unrelated business income and the payment of taxes is important, but not an issue that should dominate the operation of the business. More important is that the business earns money for the organization. The nonprofit should not become submerged in legal issues. The organization should spend its time and energy understanding the business it is undertaking and whether it can earn money for the nonprofit.

10 FUNDAMENTALS OF MARKETING

During the planning and early operating phases, the nonprofit organization will focus considerable time and energy on marketing. Many business experts describe marketing as *the* driving force behind any successful business. This chapter provides a brief introduction to the concept of marketing. The information presented here will help the organization to start thinking about how to design its business venture from a marketing perspective.

As noted previously in Chapter Six, people do not buy things they do not need. There are two types of needs. First are the needs basic to survival: food, shelter, clothing and social interaction. The second group of needs involves quality of life and lifestyle. These secondary needs include the need for recognition, the need for social status, the need for beauty, comfort, convenience or pleasure and the need for variety, stimulation or challenge.

The seller is responsible for identifying the need, designing a product or service to meet the need, informing people that a need exists, demonstrating the benefits of the product or service in addressing that need, and for persuading them to purchase it from the seller. The seller must also provide a means through which potential consumers can obtain the item.

Finally, the product or service must be priced attractively to the consumer. The best price is not always the lowest price. Sometimes a high price conveys an image of exclusivity and status not communicated by a lower price. For other items and markets, lower pricing may give a competitive advantage over the competition or encourage multiple purchases.

ELEMENTS OF MARKETING

The preceding paragraphs introduce the four fundamental elements of marketing: product, pricing promotion and distribution. The nonprofit's product must be well designed and meet a need (whether or not the consumer population is aware of the need). The product must be priced appropriately for the targeted market and for the product design. The product must be promoted so that the consuming public knows of its availability and how to obtain it. And the nonprofit must distribute the product in a way that is easy for the consumer to make the purchase.

Both new and experienced entrepreneurs make mistakes in underestimating the importance of marketing and the time required. A common error is to focus on one or two of the four elements of marketing. Most often attention is placed exclusively on the product or service for sale. The design and details of the product are critical to the business, but without considering the product in the context of the other elements of the marketing plan, the business will fail. For example, a group of low-income women created an all-purpose cleaning liquid that could do laundry, wash floors and clean windows, yet be gentle enough for shampoos and bathing. The group invested $10,000 of their own money to have large quantities of the product manufactured and packaged. The product was delivered to one of their houses, where it remains. They had never thought about promotion or distribution.

In another case, an arts organization manufactured large lawn chairs for distribution. Promotion in a national magazine generated orders. However, the organization had never considered how to ship the chairs beyond a local area. Their promotion strategy was not in line with their distribution capability.

CONSISTENCY

Consistency is a guiding principle of any marketing strategy. The element of design often relates directly to how the product will be positioned within the market. For example, a social service agency wants to establish an upscale counseling service to subsidize the services it provides to limited-income clients. The new service itself may be the same as that which the agency has been providing, but its packaging may be very different. The service may have a new name, there may be different people who deliver the service, or a different dress code may be required of the service providers.

The social service agency may have to adopt different techniques sensitive to the target population. For example, it may be necessary to modify hours to accommodate professionals. Consider convenience and status of location to a new market. Is there adequate parking nearby? Consider whether all-cash payments should be continued or billing procedures introduced.

Pricing the new counseling service is critical. Nonprofits generally underprice their services. This may be because they are unaware of their value, because they want to make their services available to as many people as possible or simply because they are afraid to ask for more. This approach may not necessarily work for the new counseling service contemplated. An image of exclusivity may make the service more attractive to a more affluent clientele, and a higher price might convey that image. The hypothetical agency wants to be competitive with similar counseling services, and it also wants to generate profit.

The social service agency must develop a promotion strategy that informs potential clients that the new counseling center exists, that it provides quality services, and that the agency is responsive to their scheduling, transportation and counseling needs. The promotion strategy must be consistent with the more exclusive image the agency is presenting. They may choose to market through free presentations in stress-related situations at corporate offices. In addition to the staff who provide the counseling services, the agency may need a sales force to implement the promotion strategy.

PRODUCT

The same marketing elements apply to selling a service or a product: product, pricing, promotion and distribution. Research conducted for the feasibility study should help in the development of a detailed marketing plan.

Be sure to consider the design, size, color, shape, taste, quality and materials of what is being sold. Should units be sold together or separately? Are multiple sales or single sales anticipated? Should follow-up servicing or second-stage additions be part of the product? All of these issues are related to the comprehensive nature of the marketing strategy.

Different types of products will require different entry strategies. There is an entry strategy for supply products and an entry strategy for demand products. A supply product is a service or product never before introduced. For example, when personal computers were first introduced, the consuming public did not understand their uses or why they needed to own one. Because of the lack of consumer awareness, little demand existed for the product when first offered, although the potential market was large.

The first responsibility in marketing a supply product is to educate the consumer, then to sell the product. The education phase of this two-step process may take a great deal of time and money, but without the educational phase, sales are impossible. If protected by patents or licensing, the profits from a supply business can be substantial.

In selling a demand product, the demand has already been established, either because the product is a basic need or because the competition has done the education work. There is no need to educate the public about what a bakery is, for example. Promotional efforts would not be focused on education, but on informing people that a new bakery has opened, where it is located, and what are its advantages over the competition. A demand business does not have the costs and risks involved in educating consumers that are present in a supply business.

PRICING

There are two primary pricing considerations: the cost to manufacture the product or deliver the service and the price the consumer is willing to pay. The total cost of the product or service is the bottom line. If an organization charges less than the product costs, the business will continually lose money; yet what determines the selling price is what the consumer is willing to pay. If the consumer will pay only less than the cost, the organization must change the product or service to lower the cost, increase the price without increasing the cost, or abandon the business concept entirely. If the consumer will pay more than the total cost (production, marketing, overhead, salaries), the organization is in a potentially profitable situation. The organization must evaluate whether the profit is reasonable once all costs are paid.

Pricing should be sensitive to, but not always confined by, the competition. The organization may be able to charge a higher price if its product or service is worth it. Or an organization may undertake a strategy of temporarily pricing below the competition to attract customers as a means of establishing itself in the market. A permanent low-price strategy also might be considered, but pricing as a competitive strategy is always susceptible to further undercutting by the competition, and the organization risks being priced out of business. This happened to a surgical supply company started by a hospital. The resulting price war drove the new supply company out of business because it was inadequately capitalized to sustain the war that they had begun.

PROMOTION

Promotion techniques can range from public relations stories in local magazines and newspapers to fliers on car windows; from radio, television, newspaper, magazine and classified advertisements to billboards, posters, balloons and airplanes trailing signs above the beach. Additional techniques include: word-of-mouth, direct mail, telephone or door-to-door solicitation; parties, samples, catalogs, brochures and trade shows; and coupons, discounting, two-for-one sales and introductory premiums. The form of promotion should support, not contradict, the image of the product or service.

DISTRIBUTION

Distribution also offers a variety of options: wholesaling versus retailing; door-to-door sales; catalog sales; commercial space; direct mail; service at home or service in an office; service by people or by computer; telephone ordering; mail distribution; even sidewalk stands. Business location may be critical to the distribution plan. Obtaining shelf space or favorable positioning for impulse purchases is an essential distribution strategy for some products. Service businesses may rely on easy consumer access.

The organization may want to use multiple forms of distribution, as well as multiple forms of promotion. Different pricing strategies may be appropriate for different geographic areas or different markets. The characteristics of the product or service may vary for different markets.

The Metropolitan Museum's successful gift shop has evolved through several distribution strategies. The shop began by selling to visitors to the museum, then expanded to mail order sales, and later opened a retail boutique in Macy's main store in New York. Recently, independent Metropolitan Museum retail stores have been opened in upscale shopping malls in New Jersey and Connecticut. Each is well designed and elegantly presented to command relatively high prices and attract an upscale consumer.

Remembering these essential elements of the marketing mix— price, product, promotion and distribution—will assist the nonprofit in thinking through the various aspects of the marketing plan. They should be used as guides when doing research or evaluating potential business ideas. Do not underestimate the importance of marketing and its impact on your entire venture.

This brief chapter is only an introduction to the wide range of options and considerations. Marketing is an area in which it may pay to call upon professional expertise and advice.

11 PRO FORMA FINANCIAL STATEMENTS

The financial statements developed by the nonprofit organization for its business are important in two ways. First, the financial statements enable potential financiers to review the fiscal plans and performance projections for the business. More importantly, the financial statements are the planning tools with which the organization can control its new business on a daily, weekly, monthly and yearly basis. The financial statements are part of both the feasibility study and the business plan for the venture.

The most important financial statements, at this stage of business development, are the start-up budget, the income statement and the cash flow analysis. Additional information about these statements is included in the detailed outline of the business plan found in Chapter 14.

At this point, the organization has not yet operated the business and has no experience on which to judge income and expenses. Instead, the nonprofit develops its financial statements by making projections based on a set of assumptions about how the business will operate. Financial statements of this type are called pro forma business financial statements. The projections are based not on experience, but on research and investigation conducted for the feasibility study or business plan.

FINANCIAL ASSUMPTIONS

The value of pro forma financial statements, to the organization and to others, depends upon the clarity of the assumptions on which the statements are based. Clearly and simply stated assumptions allow others to know the basis on which the organization has developed its figures. In addition, the organization knows the basis on which it has made decisions so that if the situation on which the assumptions were based changes, the organization can adjust its projections to reflect that change. Or if performance of the business varies from that projected, the organization can question its original assumptions and determine why performance is less or more than expected.

Examples of financial assumptions include the following: the decision of purchasing versus leasing capital equipment; the decision of purchasing versus leasing a business location; the prime interest rate; the interest rate for borrowing money; the amount of money to be borrowed; prices of supplies; salaries; benefit rates; the rate of inflation affecting operations of the business; tax rates; utility costs; insurance costs; and the rate of business growth.

The assumptions should be clearly stated. For example, it is assumed that personnel costs will increase five percent annually; or, it is assumed that taxes will be 18 percent of the net income. Clearly stated assumptions introducing the financial statements provide a record of the assumptions and a basis on which to project the business figures.

START-UP BUDGET

The start-up budget for the business operation is, in some ways, the easiest to prepare of the financial statements. The start-up budget lists and totals all costs incurred by the business before any sales are made. Included in the start-up budget are: capital budget items (list each piece of equipment with model number, source and cost); cost of acquiring a lease and any leasehold improvements; consulting or attorney's fees incurred in starting the business; early marketing costs; prototype development and testing; and any staffing or administrative costs. Most of the figures for the start-up budget, and for the other financial statements, are drawn from the research conducted for the feasibility study and business plan.

INCOME STATEMENT

The income statement is sometimes called a profit and loss statement. The income statement lists all the costs of doing business (the cost of the product or service being sold, along with operating and administrative expenses) and subtracts the total from gross sales. These statements are generally done on a monthly basis, but, during the early planning phase, the income statement covers annual projections. In most small businesses, income projections covering a three-year period are adequate.

The figures used in the income statement should be as accurate as possible. Again, the numbers come from the research for the feasibility study and the business plan. The research data and the assumptions are translated into figures used in the income statement.

The organization should also consider income ratios for businesses similar to its venture. Dun & Bradstreet and Robert Morris Associates calculate income ratios based on surveys of businesses across the country. Their ratios give average costs for particular industries (listed by SIC code) in terms of percentage of gross sales. Gross sales (total sales before any expenses) equal 100 percent. For a particular industry, average profit may be 7 percent of gross sales, advertising costs may be 3 percent of gross sales, labor costs may be 30 percent, the cost of goods sold (the product) may be 45 percent, interest payments may be 2 percent of gross sales, etc.

These ratios provide a standard against which the organization can compare and improve its financial forecasting. If the nonprofit's figures deviate too far from the industry ratio without good reason, there is probably something amiss in the organization's planning. These figures are based on businesses that have been operating successfully for some time, and as such should provide a guide for operating a financially successful business.

In preparing the income statement, it is best to err on the side of overestimating expenses. It is better to plan conservatively and overperform than to plan liberally and underperform. The organization must be thorough in listing its expenses. Among the expenses most often overlooked are interest payments on borrowed money and insurance costs. Marketing expenses generally tend to be higher than expected. And there are always expenses that cannot be foreseen. The best way to provide for unexpected expenses is to allow a liberal contingency fund as part of the income statement.

The three-year summary income statement in Figure 11.1 reveals a great deal about the product-selling business to which it applies and the assumptions used in preparing the financial statement.

- Based on the wholesale and retail sales figures, it appears that establishing a retail market will be easier than establishing a wholesale market. However, the wholesale market appears to offer more growth potential, while the retail market seems to reach a $91,000 ceiling.
- The cost of materials for this business is an extremely high 78 percent of total sales. This may be a realistic figure for a perishable food business, but it leaves little money for other operating expenses, as reflected in the gross margin. A gross margin of $13,328 in year one and $30,327 in year two is all that would be available for all other operating expenses.
- Salaries increase from 4B percent of total operating expenses in the first year to 6B percent of total operating expenses in the third year. The first year salary level of $5,000 increased to $16,000 in the third year. Does this large increase represent an attempt in the initial years to keep the entrepreneurs' salaries relatively low to provide sufficient

FIGURE 11.1: Pro Forma Income Statement

PERISHABLE FOOD BUSINESS, INC.
Pro Forma Income Statement
3 Year Summary

Income Projection	Year I	Year II	Year III
Sales			
Wholesale	$27,400	$68,800	$84,000
Retail	40,400	91,000	91,000
Bad Debt Expense	(688)	(1,598)	(1,750)
Total: Sales	67,112	158,202	173,250
Cost of Material	52,884	124,625	136,550
Variable Labor Cost	900	3,250	5,200
Cost of Goods Sold	53,784	127,875	141,750
Gross Margin	13,328	30,327	31,500
Operating Expenses:			
Utilities	1,200	1,680	1,920
Salaries	5,160	14,400	16,000
Payroll Taxes & Benefits	480	1,360	1,520
Advertising	480	720	720
Office Supplies	120	180	180
Insurance	600	600	600
Maintenance & Cleaning	240	300	300
Legal & Accounting	504	740	740
Delivery Expense	1,320	1,802	1,764
Licenses	60	60	60
Boxes, Paper, etc.	120	240	240
Telephone	600	720	720
Depreciation	480	480	480
Miscellaneous	276	400	400
Total: Operating Expenses	11,640	23,682	25,644
Other: Expenses:			
Interest (mortgage) 9.75%	2,160	2,160	2,160
Interest (loan) 10.75%	900	900	900
Total: Other Expenses	3,060	3,060	3,060
Total: All Expenses	14,700	26,742	28,704
Net Profit (loss) pre-tax	(1,372)	(3,585)	(2,796)**

**Net profit is down slightly because of an increase in salaries paid to the two partners.

Source: *Business Planning Guide*, Upstart Publishing Co., Portsmouth, NH, 1981, p. 57.

funds for other operating expenses? Even the salary of $16,000 represents a sacrifice on the part of the entrepreneurs.

- How do the entrepreneurs expect to realize a 250 percent increase in sales? Their extremely low advertising costs would have to be based on a very efficient strategy to have this kind of impact. Perhaps, the business plan says one of the entrepreneurs will act as a sales force. These estimates would be less reliable if based on a passive word-of-mouth advertising strategy.
- The 9.75 percent mortgage indicates intent to purchase a building. Unless the entrepreneurs view the real estate purchase as a significant investment in itself, they may be wiser to lease property and use the cash for other operating expenses.

The income statement is also used as a planning tool in examining certain elements of the business.

- Should the entrepreneurs eliminate the retail aspect of the business with its apparent ceiling and concentrate solely on the wholesale market? The advantages of such a change might include: less expensive space or location requirements; possibly reduced labor costs; and the sales strategy would not be split between two competing interests. Perhaps the research indicates that success in the wholesale market requires a retail outlet as well.
- Should the business focus on retailing and open other lease costs and other operating expenses. Further, it would require management of more than one site, entailing increased management responsibilities or hiring additional management personnel. On the other hand, economy of scale could be realized in purchasing, service contracts and advertising.
- Should the business aggressively build the wholesale market between the second and third years when the increase in sales drops from $40,000 to $16,000? This would probably require higher salary costs or a much higher advertising budget.
- Should the business cut the cost of its material by decreasing its quality? If the business is built on quality product, cutting quality would have a detrimental effect on the business.
- Are the operating expenses underestimated for the business? Higher actual expenses in some categories will cause serious problems for such a tightly budgeted operation.

- Should the business increase sales by raising the price of the units sold? Raising the price may reduce the number of sales. Should the price be lowered slightly to increase the number of units sold, possibly resulting in greater sales? The research may indicate that the sales and volume figures used to project total sales are sound figures and place the business in the most favorable competitive position in the marketplace.

As can be seen from this brief exercise, the income statement provides a great deal of information and is an important planning tool. The income statement does not exist independently of other research and planning. A change in one area of the business would require changes in most other figures of the income statement. A new strategy would have to be researched, and a new income statement developed, to determine if the venture as reconceived would be viable.

Once the business starts operation, comparing the projected figures of the income statement to actual figures allows the organization to monitor, control and adjust its business plan and operations to fit the situation. The income statement is a working document of great value if developed and used properly.

CASH FLOW STATEMENT

The third financial statement important at this stage in developing a new business is the pro forma cash flow statement. The reason many new businesses fail is that they run out of cash. They do not have the money to pay bills, to pay salaries and to cover other cash outflows. Employees become unsympathetic, suppliers no longer extend credit, and the utility company ultimately threatens termination of service.

Why do new businesses encounter this problem? First, they have not correctly anticipated how cash will flow in and out of their business. Second, their projections are overly optimistic, anticipating that cash will come in faster and go out slower than it does. The cash flow analysis can help solve the first issue. Only sound research and conservative planning can help with the second.

In most business, the cash generated to pay bills comes primarily from sales. Income statements may show optimistic figures, even a profit, but the venture depends on how much cash is coming in and when it will be in hand. The organization must anticipate and plan for the following: What percentage of sales will be delayed one, two or three months before receiving payment? What invoices must be paid immediately or in advance and which can be delayed? What is the collection delay on sales paid by check? What percentage of credit card sales is deducted by the credit card company? What percentage of sales will be paid through the organization's own credit system, such as an installment plan? (An installment plan requires a follow-up billing system to assure collection of funds.)

A seasonal business illustrates the problems of uncoordinated cash flow. For example, manufacturing in the bathing suit industry takes place during November, December and January, a period of high cash outlay. However, income from sales is not received until April, May, June and July. The business must have enough cash to manufacture the goods during the winter or there will be nothing to sell come spring. The spring income must be managed to sustain the corporation, or other financing must be obtained in order to manufacture the goods. Annual or monthly fluctuations occur in any business. The cash flow statement is used as a planning and controlling tool. The organization can review line-by-line where its disbursements are less or more than anticipated, and take corrective action if necessary.

A cash flow statement for the hypothetical perishable food business is shown in Figure 11.2. The cash flow statement totals cash receipts and cash disbursements and presents the difference between the two as net cash flow. The net cash flow is a monthly indication of the business's negative or positive cash flow. More important are the monthly cumulative cash flow figures. A net cash shortage of $300 a month does not seem significant, but it represents $3,600 at the end of twelve months. The amount of money needed to sustain the business is not the $300 but the cumulative figure, in this case $3,600.

In most cash flow statements, there is a bottom point representing the largest amount of cash needed by the business. After that point, the business usually improves until a positive cash flow is achieved. The bottom point is significant to business operations. It may occur fairly early in the life of the business or as late as the seventh or eighth year. Some businesses, particularly seasonal industries such as the bathing suit company, every year may have months of negative cash flow and other months of positive cash flow, with this pattern never changing, no matter how successful the business. Understanding the seasonality and cash flow patterns of the business is an important area of research for the feasibility study and business plan.

The start-up budget, the income statement and the cash flow analysis are important financial planning tools. If used as working documents, they can be of great value in planning and operating the business. Projections should be made for three to five years, and they should be calculated monthly during the first years of operation. The organization should use the information collected in its previous research, as well as the industry ratios available at a business library or through the appropriate trade as-

FIGURE 11.2: Pro Forma Cash Flow

Pro Forma Cash Flow*
PERISHABLE FOOD BUSINESS, INC.
January to December, 19__ (Fiscal Year)

	Jan	Feb	Mar	Apr	May
Cash Receipts					
Income from Sales					
Wholesale	1000	1200	1400	1600	1800
Retail	3000	3100	3100	2900	2700
Total: Cash Receipts	4000	4300	4500	4500	4500
Cash Disbursements					
Cost of Goods	3120	3354	3510	3510	3510
Variable Labor					
Advertising	100	25	25	25	25
Insurance			150		
Legal and Accounting		125			125
Delivery Expense	80	85	90	95	100
Fixed Cash Disbursement	688	688	688	688	688
Loan No. 1	145	145	145	145	145
Mortgage	250	250	250	250	250
Total Cash Disbursements	4383	4672	4858	4713	4843
Net Cash Flow	(383)	(372)	(358)	(213)	(343)
Cumulative Cash Flow	(383)	(755)	(1113)	(1326)	(1669)

Fixed Cash Disbursements	
Utilities	100
Salaries	430
Payroll Taxes & Benefits	40
Office Supplies	10
Maintenance and Cleaning	20
Licenses	5
Boxes, Paper, etc.	10
Telephone	50
Miscellaneous	23
	$688

*Assuming $8,500 working capital loan and $22,000 mortgage loan.

Source: *Business Planning Guide*, Upstart Publishing Co., Portsmouth, NH, 1981, p.72.

sociation. The nonprofit's accountant can assist the organization in preparing these financial statements and in setting up a bookkeeping and reporting system.

Examples of financial statements for retailing, service and manufacturing businesses are available in publications of the U.S. Small Business Administration. More information on financial statements can be found in

June	July	Aug	Sept	Oct	Nov	Dec	Total
2200	2400	2800	2800	3200	3300	3500	27,400
2800	3300	3700	3900	3900	4000	4000	40,400
5000	5700	6500	7000	7000	7300	7500	67,800
3900	4446	5070	5460	5460	5694	5850	52,884
		200	200	200	200	100	900
40	40	40	40	40	40	40	480
150			150			150	600
		125			125		500
110	110	120	130	130	135	135	1,320
688	688	688	688	688	688	688	8,256
145	145	145	145	145	145	145	1,740
250	250	250	250	250	250	250	3,000
5283	5679	6638	7063	6913	7277	7358	69,680
(283)	21	(138)	(63)	87	23	142	(1,880)
(1952)	(1931)	(2069)	(2132)	(2045)	(2022)	(1880)	

popular books about starting a new business. Many books on this subject can be found at the local bookstore or library.

    Examples and descriptions of balance sheets and break-even analysis, as well as additional explanations of income statements and cash flow analysis, can be found in Chapter 14.

12 THE BUSINESS PLAN

The Center for Entrepreneurial Studies at the New York University Stern School of Business recently compared the business plans and actual performance of new businesses. The businesses, financed by venture capitalists, were examined after they had begun operation. The study found that none of the operating businesses matched precisely the plans that had been prepared prior to operation. Some deviated considerably, even in the product sold and the market in which they were operating. Most had overprojected sales and growth and underprojected expenses. In all cases the businesses were not operating as planned.

Why, then, develop a business plan? The nonprofit has completed the feasibility study and carefully evaluated the information it contains. Most likely, the study has been reviewed by the board or a committee of the board, by experts in the business and by the nonprofit staff. The feasibility study has educated the nonprofit about the industry, the market and some details of the operation. The feasibility study has given the organization a sense of the options available and some criteria to be used in choosing among the options.

The business plan is a different kind of report. While the feasibility study is an educational document, the business plan presents educated choices and the actual design of the business. The feasibility study is skeptical and critical, while the business plan is positive and relatively confident. From the available options, the business plan makes choices.

The business plan describes precisely what the business is, how it will operate, who will be involved, how much it will cost, how long it will take and what kind of support is needed. Writing a business plan forces the organization to think through the various aspects of the business in detail and to make decisions in a structured way. Writing the plan involves the organization in business details it might otherwise overlook or not plan carefully. The business plan communicates to the board, the staff and potential financiers what the nonprofit is doing and how they might support the venture. The business plan outlines assumptions and specifies benchmarks against which to measure performance. These assumptions and benchmarks provide a basis on which to judge strategic decisions and changes in strategic direction.

The business plan helps nonprofits to adapt to a situation different from what they have experienced in working with government and some private funding sources. The nonprofit organization usually submits a proposal up to a year before a program begins, receives the funds, operates the program, and reports on its accomplishments a year later. Proposals and contracts are written with the expectation that what is proposed is exactly what will take place, and failure to accomplish all objectives will result in a reduction or termination of support. Nonprofits often believe they must promise more than they can deliver in order to obtain funding.

The ability to stay in business often depends on the ability to learn from mistakes, and to change. A business must change as the environment changes or else it is doomed to failure. The nonprofit board and staff must view the business plan, not as a rigid government contract or foundation proposal, but as a flexible document that stipulates a starting point from which to build. The specific details of the plan are often less important than the direction in which the business is moving and whether the business is developing in a healthy way. Timetables are artificially created; certain aspects will take longer than expected and others take less time than planned. More important than strict adherence to the business plan is responding appropriately to situations as they arise, and, of course, prudent management of the business.

Instead of using time lines, many business consultants now recommend milestone planning. In milestone planning, specific events are designated as trigger events. The business does not proceed to the next stage until a specific event takes place or a designated task is accomplished. Examples of such milestones include arranging initial financing, building production or merchandising facilities, test-marketing the product and obtaining the first major client. Using such events as triggers, plans can be structured so that funds to achieve step number two are not released until step number one has been accomplished. Milestone planning provides more control to the parent financing institution and to the organization in the operation of its business. Good milestone planning structures the evolution of the business in a rational way. Poor milestone planning can so constrain the business that it fails.

Chapter 14 provides a highly detailed outline of a business plan. Although most business plans do not contain this level of detail, it is provided to help raise all the issues that might possibly confront a nonprofit venture. A basic, less detailed outline for the business plan begins below.

Before the nonprofit starts to write its business plan, it is recommended that the people involved read several different outlines. Business plan outlines are available from the U.S. Small Business Administration and the U.S. Department of Commerce in Washington, D.C., as well as in books and in articles in business and other libraries. Outlines differ slightly in the level of detail they provide and the order in which the information is presented, but essentially the same information is presented. The nonprofit should use the outline that appears most suitable to its venture. The business plan should be written clearly and concisely, without rhetoric and without too much promotional language. The idea should sell itself with the facts presented.

The business plan should contain an executive summary, and many readers of business plans suggest tabbing key sections for easy reference.

The document should be clean and professional but not extravagant in appearance. The nonprofit staff want to make the impression that they are a group of knowledgeable business people and careful spenders. A leather-bound business plan may communicate to potential financiers that the organization's priorities are more superficial than businesslike.

BASIC BUSINESS PLAN OUTLINE

I. *Executive Summary*

A. *Business description.*
Describe in detail the product or service. Support the description with diagrams, illustrations or pictures, if available. Describe why this product or service will be a success.

B. *Marketing Summary*
Describe the targeted market segment. Describe how this market will be reached and why this strategy will be successful.

C. *Summary of Financial Statements*
State the anticipated level of sales in each of the first three years, the anticipated profit in each of the first three years and the estimated start-up capital needed. The organization may want to name key individuals involved in the business and sources and amounts of financing already committed.

II. *Statement of Objectives*
Clearly describe the product or service and why it is desirable. Include the character of the business (that is, the image presented to customers), the distinct competitive advantage of the product or service, long-range and short-range objectives for the proposed

business, sub-objectives for the proposed business, and the organization's qualifications to run the business. The organization may want to include the mix of goods and services to be produced or sold, the pricing policy and the rationale for the policy.

III. Background of Proposed Business

Briefly summarize the existing conditions in the industry, including: where the product is now used; how the product is now used; who comprises the current market; what the trends are for the industry; the major factors that influence the industry; who the consumers are; and the major trends and factors affecting the consumers.

IV. Market Description and Analysis and Market Capture Strategy

Describe the organization's primary and secondary trade areas, primary and secondary customers, major competitors, competitive advantages, anticipated market share, specific market capture strategy and sales approaches. Provide supporting evidence as necessary to justify the analysis, strategy and resulting sales estimates.

V. Technical Description of Product or Service

Describe in technically accurate language how the product works or the service is used; why the product or service is so designed; tests conducted and test results; concepts for follow-up products or services; and how the product will be produced or the service delivered.

VI. Marketing Strategy and Selling Tactics

Describe fully the targeted segment of the market. Describe in detail the distribution channels to reach this market (retailers, jobbers, wholesalers, brokers, door-to-door, mail order, party plan, etc.). Describe the share of the market the organization expects to capture and the time frame within which it expects to do so. Outline the specific selling tactics and activities the organization will use to sell the product or service, including promotional methods (direct mail, telephone sales, print advertising, radio, television, etc.). The organization may want to describe its use of a sales force or account executive. Scripts of radio spots, brochures or other promotional literature may be included in this section. Any pre-committed sales should be noted.

VII. Plan of Operations

Describe operational details such as the following: inventory on hand and inventory required; sources of supply, supplier services, turnover and important terms of supplier relationships; description of business location (proximity to customers and competitors, transportation routes, parking, etc.), and description of physical facility (necessary improvements to the facility, important zon-ing, utility or access information, layout and floor plan, flow of activity through the facility, necessary fixtures, furniture and equipment, whether they will be purchased or leased, how much they will cost, when they will be available, how they will be maintained and when they will be replaced).

VIII. Labor Force Plan

Describe production or service labor force, how employees will be recruited, trained and compensated, what their qualifications are and why this determination was made. Describe the management and administrative plan, and include an organization chart showing business functions and relationships. Identify key personnel by name, their qualifications and what they will contribute to the business. (Include resumes of key individuals in an appendix.) Describe compensation and benefit plans. The organization may want to describe additional professional services necessary to the business; these technical consultants, the attorney and accountant should be identified by name.

IX. Financial Structure

Include financial statements and the analysis of income statement, cash flow, start-up budget, a break-even analysis and, perhaps, the opening balance sheet. Provide a statement of key assumptions and a narrative explaining the figures.

Describe the approach and steps that will be taken in starting the proposed business. State how much capital is needed and the expected sources of capital. Include an analysis of the return the investor can expect and a proposed schedule for loan repayment.

X. Legal Structure

Describe the ownership structure and how the business will relate to the nonprofit corporation (whether the business is part of the nonprofit or is a separate corporation). The organization may want to discuss the flow of money between the two entities and the responsibilities of one to the other.

XI. Supporting Documents

Include legal documents and supporting data, such as leases, equipment and refurbishing estimates, architectural drawings, results of product or service marketing tests, lists of capital equipment, packaging and shipping information. The organization may want to include price schedules here or in an appendix.

The business plan should anticipate and answer the questions of its readers. It should be realistic, not overly optimistic. If possible, the organization should involve the future manager of the business in writing the plan, so that the manager can incorporate his or her experience and preferences. With board approval of the business plan, the nonprofit organization is ready to seek seed capital from prospective funders and to implement its venture.

13 FINANCING OPTIONS

Once the organization has completed its business plan, the next step is to seek the financing necessary to start and operate the venture. The nonprofit needs funds with which to capitalize the business and funds to manage its cash flow on an ongoing basis, and the business plan shows exactly how much money is needed and when. Cash requirements do not all occur at the same time. One business venture may start with minimal capital but then need funds to expand operations one or two years later. Another business may need substantial funds to subsidize its cash flow in the fall but not in the spring. Knowing the venture's needs and the timing of those needs is the first step in developing a financing plan.

Approximately 75 percent of the hundreds of thousands of businesses started each year in the United States are started with the entrepreneur's own money. There is no borrowed money, venture capital or outside financing involved at all. The money comes from savings accounts, second mortgages, insurance policies or sympathetic relatives. Another 18 percent of new businesses are started with some borrowed or invested capital but primarily with the individual's money. Only less than seven percent of new businesses are financed primarily with outside investment capital.

In many ways, nonprofit corporations have an advantage over the individual entrepreneur in obtaining investment capital. The nonprofit corporation has a financial track record, proven management capability and a public reputation that make its proposal more attractive. Also, the nonprofit is possibly in a position to put up some of the capital required or to put up collateral to guarantee an investment. However, most nonprofit corporations have little experience in operating a business in the commercial marketplace. Nonprofits may have restricted assets, cash flow problems, no financial plan, assets owned by others or weak relationships with their financial institutions.

The greater the financial strength of the nonprofit when it seeks financing for its business, the better the chances are of obtaining financing. In addition, a positive ongoing relationship with a financial institution can lead to the institution being a financing source or a reference, if necessary.

Nonprofits may seek public funds or private grants as a means of subsidizing the business operation. For example, a local manpower program may pay half the salary of employees hired by the business. This type of funding may be a valuable source of start-up capital or a means of moderating cash flow problems in the early days of the business. However, a business is doomed to fail if its financial plan relies solely on subsidies. Grants, special programs and low interest loans do not last forever. The business must be planned and built based on current and projected fair market costs. If the nonprofit is going to take advantage of such subsidies, it should do so with full awareness of their limitations. In addition, the time frame of a government contract or grant and their performance requirements may not be compatible with the business time frame.

A nonprofit organization that establishes its business as a separate for-profit corporation has the following financing options to consider:

- Mobilization of the organization's internal resources
- Grants and donations for which the organization may have limited or no obligations to the grantor or donor
- Borrowed money, or debt financing, that carries an obligation to repay the money with interest at a specified time
- Equity financing, in which the organization sells shares of the business to raise needed capital
- Sale of goods or services

If the business venture is not a separate for-profit corporation, the same options are available, with the exception of equity financing.

MOBILIZE INTERNAL RESOURCES

Many nonprofits capitalize their business ventures through internal resources. In fact, the organization may have to commit its own money to the venture to convince other investors to take the venture seriously. Investors and financial institutions normally require an investment by the entrepreneur of 15 percent to 50 percent. In addition, investing some of the organization's money provides increased control over the venture.

The nonprofit corporation may be able to raise new funds through traditional means or by freeing funds locked in by its internal structure. Examples of the latter follow below:

(1) Raise funds by sponsoring activities such as theater or sports events, food sales, auctions or raffles, dinners, or award ceremonies and

other techniques nonprofits traditionally employ to raise funds. Fundraising might include special bequests or deferred giving specifically earmarked for investment in the venture.

(2) Examine the nonprofit's cash management to identify cost centers and to track monthly or weekly cash flow. The organization may be able to accelerate receivables, decelerate payables, predict its cash flow more accurately and, as a result, capture excess funds.

(3) Convert assets to cash by, for example, mortgaging a building, selling equipment or vehicles from an obsolete program or cashing in or drawing upon stocks or certificates of deposit.

(4) Economize in various ways, such as recycling to save on supplies; bidding the nonprofit's insurance package; reducing inventory; or switching accounting or legal firms. For example, one hospital corporation stopped providing free coffee to its employees and saved $40,000 a year. Perhaps employees would sacrifice a penny a mile on reimbursement of travel expenses for a period of time.

(5) Prioritize the organization's activities and postpone or possibly eliminate certain expenses, such as a staff retreat, attending a convention or buying a new typewriter. A nonprofit may shut down a losing division or an underutilized facility in order to raise capital.

(6) Leverage existing capital by using existing cash and assets as guarantees or collateral to borrow money. The nonprofit may simply elect to invest in or loan unrestricted funds to the new venture.

DEBT FINANCING

An organization that has mobilized sufficient internal resources may want to borrow the balance of funds needed for the business. Borrowing funds is called debt financing. The repayment of the principal and the interest must be calculated in the cash flow planning for the business, but these payments are commonly ignored among new entrepreneurs. Changes in interest rates charged on loans also affect a business's cash flow.

The nonprofit might approach its own bank, a large commercial bank, the Small Business Administration or a foundation-sponsored investment program to borrow money. The lender will seek certain assurances and guarantees in exchange for the loan, a bank is a profit-making corporation, and even foundations and government lenders must meet their obligations. In order to do so, the lender will structure the loan to require one or more of the following:

- The lender may require collateral—something valued in excess of the loan amount—to secure the loan. It may be cash collateral held in a certificate of deposit, property or securities, such as stocks and bonds. The nonprofit may use its own assets to collateralize a loan or it may turn to individuals or special programs run by foundations or government for the collateral. If real property is used to collateralize the loan, the lender will require assurance that the property is insured.

- The lender will be interested in earning as high an interest rate as possible. It may choose a variable rate that fluctuates with the prime rate or other market interest rates. In addition, the lender may set a lower limit, or floor, on the interest rate but not set an upper limit, or ceiling.
- The lender may be interested in a short-term loan to be repaid as quickly as possible. Typical loans last from three to seven years. The schedule of payments may begin immediately with both principal and interest repaid throughout the life of the loan.
- The lender may want to be able to call the note—that is, require full payment on demand with short notice—at its discretion.
- The lender may want a way to control and oversee the operation of the business, such as selection and review of management staff, open audit review, a seat on the board, or control of the business assets until the loan is repaid.
- The lender may want to link release of funds to performance, such as a sales or inventory level.
- Periodic financial reports using a format established by the lender may be required.
- The lender may also apply various fees and commissions to the loan, including an application fee, an administrative fee, closing costs and points (percentage charges).

The lender may look for other means of maintaining security and control over the loan. In any case, the lender's interest is not to constrain the organization's ability to operate its business but to assure that the funds will be repaid in a timely manner.

As the borrower, the nonprofit organization is seeking a low interest rate, a long-term loan, no points, total control over the cash, deferred interest and deferred principal repayment—basically the opposite of lender's interests. It is unlikely that the lender will impose all the available restrictions, but the nonprofit should expect a combination of controls over any loan. In negotiating the loan, the nonprofit may be able to persuade the lender to drop certain requirements.

Banks and other lenders usually employ loan criteria based on the level of risk. Unlike consumer lending, commercial loans are not tightly regulated by federal or state laws. Open negotiations between the nonprofit and the lender determine the terms and restrictions applicable to the loan. The nonprofit must be sure to build the conditions of the loan into its business plan and its cash flow statements.

EQUITY FINANCING

Another investment strategy is to attract investors to the business venture. Investors are risk takers who buy stock in the corporation in hope of realizing a capital gain as well as dividends on their investment. Risk takers know there is no guaranteed return on their investment.

If the nonprofit operates its business as a separate private corporation, it may sell stock in the business to anyone it chooses. The relationship with investors is subject to negotiation; however, the nonprofit is responsible for full disclosure about the business to potential investors. A lawyer should assist the nonprofit in complying with state and Securities Exchange Commission laws.

Similar to lenders, equity investors look for protection of their investment and other indicators of a sound venture.

- Investors look for a good track record on the part of the individuals involved and, if possible, a good track record on the part of the business.
- Investors look for guarantees, such as convertible stocks, which allow the investor to convert equity to debt, or a guaranteed first position on the assets, in the event of bankruptcy.
- Investors are interested in limited liability so that the debts of the corporation are not the responsibility of shareholders.
- Depending on the level of investment in the corporation, investors may want management approval or control.
- Depending on the level of investment, investors may want open access to the financial records of the business.
- Investors may want seats on the board of directors of the business, and may want the majority of board positions to be held by investors.
- Investors have the right to vote for the board of directors and for policy changes in the firm.
- Investors want a high return on their investment.
- Investors want first preference on dividend distribution.
- Investors want periodic reports on the financial standing of the business.

In most situations the nonprofit organization wants to maintain control of its business corporation. If the nonprofit sells stock to capitalize its venture, it is selling partial ownership and, therefore, partial control of its business. In selling more than fifty percent of a small corporation, the nonprofit loses control. Even sales of lesser percentages dilute control and may make decision making difficult.

THE BUSINESS LIFE CYCLE

The likelihood of obtaining financing through debt financing, equity financing or grants is related to stage of its evolution that the business venture has reached with financing is sought: concept, development, growth or maturity. The receptivity of lenders, investors and grantors varies according to the stage of the business life cycle, as illustrated in Figure 13.1.

The first stage of the business life cycle is the conceptual stage. At this point in the planning process, the organization has its business idea, the preliminary feasibility study may be completed, and the nonprofit is seeking financing for a thorough feasibility study and business plan.

Debt financing is highly unlikely at this stage of the business cycle. There is no product, no inventory, no track record and no cash flow. There is very little to assure repayment of debt. Debt financing would be feasible only through a well-collateralized personal loan, virtually unrelated to the business.

Equity financing at the conceptual stage is impossible. The nonprofit does not have a corporation in which to sell shares, and there is nothing to be financed.

FIGURE 13.1: Probability of Financing at Various Stages of the Business Life Cycle

STAGE OF BUSINESS LIFE CYCLE	SOURCE OF FINANCING		
	DEBT FINANCING	EQUITY FINANCING	GRANT FINANCING
CONCEPT	Unlikely	Impossible	Good
DEVELOPMENT	Possible	Possible	Possible
GROWTH	Very Good	Very Good	Possible
MATURITY	Excellent	Unlikely	Impossible

Grant financing, however, is possible. Some foundations and government programs give money to nonprofit organizations for preparing a feasibility study and business plan. Grants of $20,000 to $35,000 for this purpose are worthy of serious consideration.

The second stage of the business life cycle is the developmental stage. If planning to do so, the nonprofit has established a subsidiary corporation, its business plan is complete, and its board and management staff are in place. The organization has not yet sold any product or established a cash flow. It is looking for start-up funds.

At this stage, the business has no track record on which a lender could evaluate its ability to repay a loan, and the business has no assets to put up as collateral. The possibility of getting a loan at this stage is greater than at the conceptual stage, but not promising. It would depend primarily on board or staff personal guarantees, or the loan guarantee of another organization, a government program (such as the Small Business Administration) or a foundation. The loan would be evaluated based on the business plan, the management team and the guarantees.

Equity financing at the developmental stage is possible if the venture has a strong board, a good business plan and a strong management team. With no performance record, it would be difficult for investors to evaluate the potential for success. Those most likely to invest in a business at this stage would be risk takers looking for a high return or sympathetic family members, friends and associates. Investors would need to understand that they might never see their money again, but if the company grows rapidly and the value of the stock increases, they would realize a large capital gain on their risk.

Grant financing is also possible at the developmental stage. Foundations may be reluctant if the venture is run as a separate profit-making corporation. For foundations to invest in a nonprofit or a for-profit business, the activity must advance the foundation's mission. Many ventures do support foundation missions by serving or employing a particular population or by revitalizing a specific community. Government grants may also be available for ventures meeting this kind of criteria.

The third stage of the business life cycle is the growth stage. The nonprofit organization has been operating its business for some time, sales are increasing and the business is gaining a stronger position in the market. The business may have inventory or other assets that can be used as collateral. In addition, the business has credit ratings, financial records and management experience to be evaluated.

The probability of borrowing money at this stage is very good. The lender will be concerned with the ability of the business to repay the loan, with particular attention to the loan's impact on cash flow. The lender will also be concerned about the level of debt already assumed by the business. A business built on debt may be ideal for the entrepreneur who has little of his or her own money at stake, but a heavy debt burden threatens the venture's cash flow and, in turn, the lender's position.

Selling stock for equity financing or for underwriting expansion is a strong possibility during the growth stage. The risks of the brand-new business have been assumed by others, and the venture is strong and still growing, a good position from which to negotiate favorable equity financing. Investors still have an opportunity for capital gain on their investment and feel confident about the performance to date. Many companies choose to sell stock to the public at this stage of the business life cycle.

Grant financing at this stage is less likely, although still possible. Most grant financing would be for expansion activities related to increasing employment of a particular population or stabilizing a specific economically distressed community. More likely than grants would be government or foundation loans for these purposes.

The fourth stage of the business life cycle is maturity. The business is stable and growing at roughly the same rate as the Gross National Product. It may be seeking funds to maintain its market position, to replace existing equipment, to launch an advertising campaign, to bridge a seasonal cash flow problem or to secure a new plant.

The probability of debt financing at this stage is excellent. The business has a track record, solid cash flow, assets and inventory. If the current debt level is not excessive, securing debt financing should be relatively easy. Many lending institutions extend letters of credit (short-term loans for ongoing operations) to mature businesses.

Equity financing of a mature business is unlikely. The opportunity for capital gains are limited to current stakeholders, who are receiving regular dividends from the corporation and have little motivation to dilute their ownership. Obtaining grants for a mature business is even less likely.

POSSIBLE FINANCING SOURCES

When seeking financing, the nonprofit must think positively. Each individual corporation and foundation is a potential contributor, grantor, lender or investor, and the organization must be prepared to pursue every available avenue of financing. A bank may not be willing to make a grant, but it may be receptive to extending a collateralized loan or making an investment as part of its corporate portfolio.

Approaches to different financing sources require the preparation of different documents: a proposal for a grant, a loan application for a loan and a prospectus for an equity investment.

It is best to start the search for financing with people who are familiar and sympathetic to the organization. They know the nonprofit's reputation for quality and financial stability. These people can introduce other potential donors and investors.

In the search for financing, the nonprofit should consider the following sources: board members, staff members, friends and relatives, other nonprofits, clients, donors, suppliers, local businesses, large corporations, unions, professional associations, the Chamber of Commerce, local religious institutions, local politicians, current funders, foundation program-related investments (PRI) and national and regional investment corporations, such as the Local Initiative Support Corporation (LISC) and the National Rural Development & Finance Corporation.

Sources of advice and technical assistance, as well as financing, are numerous. Loan guarantees may be obtained from certain foundations, such as the Piton Foundation in Denver and the New York Community Trust. The Enterprise Foundation provides technical assistance to new businesses, especially those related to housing. Other possible sources of both financing and assistance include: pension trusts, insurance companies, community development corporations, the U.S. Small Business Administration, small business investment corporations, minority business investment corporations, local development corporations, business assistance centers, the Service Corps of Retired Executives (SCORE) and the National Executive Service Corps. In addition, local banks and savings and loan associations, credit unions, local business schools; and federal, state and local government agencies involved in economic development, community development, business relations, enterprise zones and tourism are potential sources of assistance. Governmental offices responsible for vocational rehabilitation, education, health and human services, veteran services, women refugee services, transportation and job creation also may be interested in the business venture.

Success in the search for financing depends upon the organization's commitment to finding it and upon the quality of the business plan. The New York Community Trust and the Ford Foundation, both of which finance nonprofit business ventures, have been frustrated in the past in their attempts to distribute funds by the poor quality of the proposals and business plans they have received. If the nonprofit organization has done its work well, has a good plan and a good team, there is good reason to believe it can obtain financing.

To make a difficult financing situation easier, a nonprofit may want to conduct a trial operation of its business on a very small scale to demonstrate its seriousness to potential investors. This limited track record could serve as illustration of the organization's cash flow, marketing strategy or investment potential. Financing limitations may force the organization to re-evaluate elements of its plan or implementation strategy. Initiating the venture with less capital than originally planned or seeking additional financing after commencing operation should not necessarily defeat a sound business idea. Use your business plan as a management tool during your search for financing. But be careful not to modify your plan so much that it becomes unfeasible or to start with such limited financing that failure is inevitable.

Financing, like fundraising, is a time-consuming task. But the payoff is usually there when the right efforts have been made.

14 THE BUSINESS PLAN—A DETAILED RESEARCH AND PLANNING GUIDE

A successful business requires: (1) a business opportunity; (2) technical know-how; (3) adequate financing; and (4) the right manager for the business. The following pages, listing questions and issues you should consider when researching and evaluating a new venture, constitute a detailed outline for a business plan. The list has evolved over a number of years and has built upon many business planning guides. Particular tribute is due to one anonymous author from whom many of the lengthy lists of questions were drawn.

The business plan answers such questions as: What is the business? Are there customers for the business? What sales volume will the business generate? What gross margin can it achieve? How can the business operate to generate estimated sales? Is the business financially feasible?

THE AREAS OF RESEARCH FOR A BUSINESS PLAN

Item I. Business Description and Product Definition

A. Specific goods, merchandise and/or services to be produced or sold

B. Mix of goods, merchandise and/or services to be produced or sold

C. Pricing policy, prices planned plus the method and rationale for determining policy and prices

Item II. Market Description and Analysis of Market Capture Strategy

A. Primary and secondary trade areas

B. Current and potential trade area sales volume plus evidence supporting estimates

C. Current and potential trade area customer categories and individuals, including numbers and purchasing power plus evidence supporting estimates

D. Major competitors, including location, products, customers, market share, competitive advantages, sales and market percentage, growth potential and analysis of how they compete

E. Market capture strategy, including competitive advantages, advertising policy, advertising planned, method and rationale for determining policy and advertising, plus customer conveniences

F. Potential customer categories and individuals, including method and rationale for determining categories and individuals, plus any written purchasing commitments

Item III. Inventory List

A. Type, quality and quantity inventory on hand (if any)

B. Type, quality and quantity inventory required

C. List narrative, including method and rationale for determining requirements, sources of supply, supplier services, proposed business/supplier legal relationship, delivery time and projected turnover explanation

D. Cost of purchase as a figure and percentage of annual projected sales, plus minimum orders, credit terms and freight or delivery costs (if any)

Item IV. Location Description

A. Address, area characteristics, notable features and zoning

B. Proximity to customers, competitors, complementary businesses, inventory suppliers, labor and personnel supply; transportation routes for customers, inventory, labor, personnel, and distribution or delivery

C. Expansion potential explanation

Item V. Physical Facility Description

A. Land lot and building size

B. Space and/or suitability for:
   1. customer and vehicle access and/or entry, parking and loading
   2. inventory storage and movement
   3. fixtures, furniture, machinery and equipment
   4. utilities
   5. production sales and/or service functions, labor and supervisors
   6. management and administrative functions and personnel
   7. merchandise display (if any)
   8. compliance with federal, state and local laws and codes
   9. security
   10. insurance

11. expansion potential

C. Cost of purchase for use as a figure and percentage of total annual capital costs plus renovation costs (if any)

Item VI. Layout and Flow Plan

A. Layout and floor plan copy

B. Layout and flow plan narrative, including method and rationale for determining design and expansion potential explanation

Item VII. Fixtures, Furniture, Machinery and Equipment List

A. New or used fixtures, furniture, machinery and equipment on hand (if any)

B. New or used fixtures, furniture, machinery and equipment required (if any)

C. List narrative, including function, method and rationale for determining requirements, source of supply, supplier services, delivery time and expansion potential explanation

D. Cost of purchase or use as a figure and percentage of total capital or annual costs plus credit terms and installation costs (if any)

Item VIII. Legal Documents for Physical Facility Fixtures, Furniture, Machinery and Equipment

A. Purchase and sale agreements (if any)

B. Leases (if any)

C. Lease/purchase agreements (if any)

D. Renovations estimates, bids and contracts (if any)

E. Installation estimates, bids and contracts (if any)

Item IX. Labor and Supervisory Force Plan

A. Production, sale and/or service, labor and supervisory force schedule, including functions, numbers, training necessary and compensation type and rate

B. Schedule narrative, including method and rationale for determining requirements, recruitment strategy, training program planned (if any) and expansion potential explanation

C. Cost of payroll, payroll taxes and fringe benefits (if any) as a figure and percentage of total annual costs, plus training costs (if any)

Item X. Management and Administrative Personnel Plan

A. Management and administrative personnel schedule, including functions, numbers, training necessary and compensation type and rate

B. Schedule narrative, including method and rationale for determining requirements, brief resumes for key personnel, recruitment strategy for remaining personnel, training program planned (if any) and expansion potential explanation

C. Cost of payroll, payroll taxes and fringe benefits (if any) as a figure and percentage of total annual costs, plus training costs (if any)

Item XI. Professional Services and Technical Assistance Plan

A. Professional services and technical assistance schedule, including functions and compensation type and rate

B. Schedule narrative, including method and rationale for determining requirements and identity of professionals and/or technical assistance resources

C. Cost of professional services and technical assistance as a figure and percentage of total annual costs

Item XII. Organization and Ownership Description

A. Legal structure

B. Identity of partners or corporate officers, board members and major (10 percent or more ownership) stockholders (if any), brief resumes for partners or key officers, plus categories, number and par value of stock (if any)

Item XIII. Acquisition or Franchise Documents

A. Purchase and sale agreement (if any)

B. Previous owner financing agreement (if any)

C. Franchise agreement (if any)

Item XIV. Financial Statements and Analyses

A. Statement of financial requirements, monthly and annual for first year, plus annual second- and third-year projected income statements and cash flow analyses and an opening balance sheet

B. Document narrative, including method and rationale for determining key projected figures

This outline can be divided into four primary areas to be researched and evaluated:

- The Market Analysis
- The Product and Sales Assessment
- The Technical and Operational Plan
- The Financial Analysis

On the following pages, sections of the plan are explored in greater detail, providing a list of specific questions and issues you may wish to research for your business. Don't skip questions that are hard to answer or that provide negative answers; dealing with these issues early on may be a key to success. At the same time, don't become bogged down on trivial, insignificant items. The list is provided to help you be aware of the range of issues that you may need to consider for your business.

MARKET ANALYSIS

The market analysis helps you to determine if there are sufficient customers for the business. It should assess the following:

- what the business sells
- trade area
- trade area sales volume (market)
- trade area customers
- trade area competition
- competitive advantages
- market captive strategy
- probable customers
- estimated sales volume

Systematically answering all of the market analysis questions below will help you to assess your market and plan your market strategy thoughtfully.

Market Analysis Questions

Group I. Product Definition

What is the nature of the business? What does the business sell? What goods, merchandise and/or services will be the product of the business? If the business is an acquisition, will its nature change? If so, how and why will it differ?

Group II. Trade Area

Who are the customers for the business? What is their profile? Where do the potential customers live or do business? To what geographic area will the business distribute or deliver goods, merchandise and/or services? How far will customers travel by car and on foot to buy what the business sells? What portion of the geographic area identified will be the primary trade area for the business? What part will be the secondary trade area? If the business is an acquisition, will its primary and secondary trade areas change? If so, how and why will they differ?

Group III. Sales Volume of the Market

What sales volume does the trade area generate for similar goods, merchandise and/or services? How much growth potential exists? Where and why does it exist? How much is sales volume likely to grow? Why? If the business is an acquisition, will trade area volume growth affect its sales? If so, how and why? If not, why not?

Group IV. Trade Area Customers

Who in the trade area buys similar goods, merchandise and/or services? What categories of customers with how much purchasing power can be identified? What major individual customers with how much purchasing power can be identified? Are they repeat purchasers? If so, how often? Within categories, what growth potential exists. For individual customers, what growth potential exists? If the business is an acquisition, will its customers change? If so, how and why will they differ?

Group V. Competition

What businesses sell similar goods, merchandise and/or services? Where are these businesses located relative to each other and the proposed location for the business? What does each major competitor sell? Which customers does each competitor attract? Do these businesses attract new customers to the area or draw customers and sales away from each other? Will their presence add to or detract from the sales volume the business can achieve? What share of the market does each control? How much potential for increased sales and market percentage does each have? What services does the competition offer to customers? What plans does the competition have for expansion or diversification? What marketing and sales strategies does the competition employ? What are the competition's start-up history, operating requirements and profitability? If the business is an acquisition, will its competition change? If so, how and why will it differ?

Group VI. Competitive Advantage

What competitive advantages does each major competitor have? Do the keys to their success include location, prices, quality, selection, merchandising, advertising, personnel, distribution or delivery methods or time or customer service? Which of these or other factors represent their most significant competitive advantages? If the business is an acquisition, will its competitive advantages change? If so, how and why will they differ?

Group VII. Market Capture Strategy

How will the business capture a share of the market? From which competitors will it draw customers and sales? What untapped categories of customers with how much purchasing power can it attract? What major individual customers with how much purchasing power can it create? How and why can it draw the competition's customers and create new individual customers? What share of the market can it capture? If the business is an acquisition, will its market capture strategy and share of the market change? If so, how and why will they differ?

Group VIII. Probable Business Customers

What specific customer categories or major individual customers can be identified as probable patrons for the business? Why is each probable? What form does the purchasing commitment of each individual customer take?

Group IX. Estimated Business Sales

How much will probable customers buy in the first and later years of business operations? What evidence supports sales estimates for each customer category and individual customer? When will each buy? Roughly, how much sales volume will the business do monthly or seasonally during the first year? How much volume will it do annually for the first three years? If the business is an acquisition, will its monthly and annual sales volume change? If so, how and why will it differ?

PRODUCT AND SALES ASSESSMENT

The sales plan helps to develop estimates for sales volume and the cost of goods sold. The product and sales assessment answers the questions: What sales volume will the business generate? What gross margin can it achieve? What advertising and sales promotion plans to support the sales plan are necessary? What amount of raw materials, merchandise and/or supplies inventory are required? The figures developed here become the basis for determining many of the operating requirements of the business.

The product and sales assessment should examine the following:
- the specific goods, merchandise and/or services the business produces or sells
- its pricing policy and prices
- its advertising, marketing and sales strategy
- customer conveniences it provides
- revenue generated through sales (sales volume)
- inventory required
- inventory turnover
- suppliers
- cost of purchasing or producing inventory (cost of goods sold)
- the level of waste, pilferage, rejections and impact on cost of goods sold

Product and Sales Assessment Questions

Group I. Product Definition and Mix

What goods, merchandise and/or services (e.g., quality, style, size, etc.) will the business sell? How much of each type of item will the business sell?

Group II. Pricing Policy and Prices

What will the business pricing policy be? What mark-ups, mark-downs, discounts, etc., will the business use? How will this policy apply to each type of item it sells? What prices will the business charge for each type of item it sells? Will there be introductory prices that will change over time? Will there be different prices for different classes of customers? Will there be sales to clear inventory? What image is being communicated through pricing? Is this consistent with product design and the marketing and sales strategy?

Group III. Advertising, Marketing and Sales Strategy

What will the advertising and marketing policy of the business be? Will it advertise high price, low price, high mark-up, low mark-up, discount, loss leader or specials items? Which media will it use to advertise? What potential customers will it try to reach? How much will it pay for each medium it uses? Which specific items will the business advertise? How and when will it advertise each item? What marketing approaches will the business use to create awareness of its services and products? Is free media and public relations a viable strategy? What about samples and promotions? How will the sales be made once interest is created?

Group IV. Customer Conveniences

What customer conveniences will the business provide? Will it extend credit? If so, on what terms? Will it accept credit cards? Will it provide free or nominal-charge delivery, one-day service or free customer parking? Will it accept telephone orders? Will it stay open after normal business hours at night or on Sunday? Will the conveniences provided influence who buys, which items sell and total sales volume? If so, what will their impact be?

Group V. Sales Revenue Volume

How much sales revenue will each type of item generate for the business? When will each type of item produce its share of total revenue? What will monthly sales volume total during the first year? What will first-year volume be? What will later-year volume be?

Group VI. Inventory Level and Mix
> How much *beginning inventory* and average inventory will the business carry for each type of item that it sells? What will the total beginning inventory be? What will the total average inventory be? What will the *ending inventory* be?

Group VII. Inventory Turnover
> How often will the inventory for each item turn over? Will inventory items turn over at differing rates depending on the time of year? How often will total inventory turn over?

Group VIII. Inventory Suppliers
> Who will supply the inventory for each item the business sells? How does each supplier compare with others who supply similar items? What is each supplier's reputation in the trade? What are his order and delivery procedures? Does he require minimum-size orders? Does he deliver at the time specified? Is the quality of what he supplies consistent? Is he unreliable in any way? What extra services or technical assistance will he provide? Will he help the business price or advertise the items it sells? Is he willing to act on behalf of the business with other suppliers or parties with whom the business must deal? Will he go out of his way to make the business a success? Does he want and need the business as a customer?

Group IX. Inventory Costs/Cost of Goods Sold
> How much does each supplier charge for each type of item he supplies? How do his prices compare to other suppliers? Does he give volume discounts, cost rebates, advertising credits or any other cost breaks to his buyers? If so, what cost breaks will he give the business? How do these compare with breaks offered by other suppliers? Does he extend credit? If so, how much credit on what terms? What credit will he extend? What form does his credit commitment take? How does his credit and terms offer compare with offers from other suppliers? What will the business pay for inventory? When will it have to pay?

Group X. Waste, Pilferage, Rejections and Returns
> How much will waste, pilferage, customer rejections, returns and other factors inherent in the production and sales process add to the cost of goods sold? What will be the total cost of goods sold?

TECHNICAL AND OPERATIONAL PLAN

The technical and operational plan examines how the business is organized and functions to generate estimated sales. It will examine:
- the physical facility

- the layout or flow plan
- fixtures, furniture, machinery and equipment
- the labor and supervisory force
- management and administrative personnel
- professional services and technical assistance

Developing this plan often involves examining possible alternatives, exploring promising ones, examining trade-offs among the most promising alternatives and finally selecting one. Each requirement implies a cost, and every cost affects the total financing needed, annual expenses or both. This obviously affects the bottom line. As each item is examined, consider its impact upon previous decisions and the impact of previous decisions upon it. The technical and operational plan represents a complex set of interrelated alternatives.

Technical and Operational Plan Questions
1) FACILITY PLAN
Group I. Requirements for the Physical Facility
A. Where should the business locate with respect to:
 1. zoning
 2. customers
 3. complementary businesses and competitors
 4. inventory suppliers
 5. labor and personnel supply
 6. transportation routes for customers, inventory, labor, personnel and distribution or delivery
 7. expansion potential

B. How much space and what structural features does the business require for:
 1. customer and vehicle access and/or entry, parking and loading
 2. inventory storage and movement
 3. fixtures, furniture, machinery and equipment installation, use, maintenance and repairs
 4. electricity, heat, air conditioning, venting, water and waste disposal
 5. production, sales and/or service functions, labor and supervisors
 6. management and administrative functions and personnel
 7. merchandise display
 8. compliance with federal, state and local laws and codes
 9. security

THE BUSINESS PLAN RESEARCH AND PLANNING GUIDE   113

   10. insurance
   11. expansion potential
  C. What are the trade-offs among space and structural suitability factors identified?
  D. What are the trade-offs among:
     1. sales
     2. location
     3. physical facility space and structural features

Group II. Costs of the Physical Facility
  A. Is it better to purchase, lease or lease/purchase the physical facility?
  B. Assuming that each ownership option is open, how do physical facility alternatives compare in:
     1. front money, total fixed and working capital required
     2. institutional financing availability and terms
     3. owner financing or credit availability and terms
     4. basic cost per month and year for financing payments or rent
     5. real estate tax costs
     6. facility renovations costs
     7. maintenance and repairs costs
     8. utilities costs
     9. security costs
     10. insurance costs
     11. actual working life and useful life for tax purposes
     12. depreciation deductions
     13. total effect on monthly and annual net income and cash flow
     14. capacity expansion costs
  C. If the facility is purchased, what cost-risk factors are written in the mortgage relative to:
     1. late payment penalties
     2. payment acceleration
     3. foreclosure
  D. If the facility is leased, what risk factors are written in the lease relative to:
     1. late payment penalties
     2. rent and tax escalation
     3. renovations and regular repairs
     4. damage or loss
     5. termination conditions

6. options to renew

E. If the facility is lease/purchased, what cost-risk factors are written in the lease/purchase agreement relative to:
   1. late payment penalties
   2. renovations and regular repairs
   3. damage or loss
   4. termination conditions
   5. option to purchase or renew

F. What are the trade-offs among:
   1. sales
   2. physical facility alternatives
   3. fixed and working capital required, annual costs plus cost risk factors

Group III. Requirements for Fixtures, Furniture, Machinery and Equipment

A. What production, sales or service functions must fixtures, furniture, machinery and equipment perform?

B. What performance standards must fixtures, furniture, machinery and equipment meet?

C. Which fixture, furniture, machinery and equipment alternatives have the capacity required to perform these functions?

D. What fixtures, furniture, machinery and equipment are required by:
   1. federal and state labor practices and safety laws
   2. state and local health, sanitation, fire and building codes

Group IV. Evaluating Fixtures, Furniture, Machinery and Equipment

A. What fixtures, furniture, machinery and equipment must be new? Which can be used?

B. How do fixture, furniture, machinery and equipment alternatives compare in
   1. size
   2. efficiency
   3. adaptability
   4. strength and durability
   5. installation, use, maintenance and repair ease
   6. parts and replacements availability
   7. capacity expansion potential

THE BUSINESS PLAN RESEARCH AND PLANNING GUIDE   115

   C. How do fixture alternatives compare in:
      1. employee numbers required for use
      2. reliability
      3. attractiveness
   D. How do furniture alternatives compare in attractiveness and comfort?
   E. How do machinery and equipment alternatives compare in:
      1. employee numbers required to operate
      2. skills and experience required to operate
      3. reliability
      4. safety

Group V. Sources of Supply
   A. What suppliers carry required fixtures, furniture, machinery and equipment?
   B. How do suppliers compare in:
      1. quality
      2. order and delivery procedures and time
      3. installation, maintenance and repairs service
      4. parts and replacement guarantees
      5. reliability
      6. extra services or technical assistance
      7. costs

Group VI. Costs of Fixtures, Furniture, Machinery and Equipment
   A. Is it better to purchase, lease or lease/purchase fixtures, furniture, machinery and equipment?
   B. Assuming that each ownership option is open, how do feasible fixtures, furniture, machinery and equipment alternatives compare in:
      1. front money, total fixed and working capital required
      2. institutional financing availability and terms
      3. supplier credit availability and terms
      4. basic cost per month and year for financing payments or rent
      5. facility renovations costs
      6. installation, maintenance, repairs and parts costs
      7. insurance costs
      8. actual working life and useful life for tax purposes
      9. *depreciation* deductions
      10. replacement costs
      11. total effect on monthly and annual net income and cash flow

12. capacity expansion costs
C. If fixtures, furniture, machinery and equipment are term-purchased, what cost-risk factors are in the purchase and sale agreement or chattel mortgage relative to:
   1. late payment penalties
   2. payment acceleration
   3. foreclosure or repossession
D. If fixtures, furniture, machinery and equipment are leased, what cost-risk factors are in the lease relative to:
   1. late payment penalties
   2. *rent escalation*
   3. regular repairs
   4. damage or loss
   5. termination conditions
   6. options to renew
E. If fixtures, furniture, machinery and equipment are lease/purchased, what cost risk factors are in the lease/purchase agreement relative to:
   1. late payment penalties
   2. regular repairs
   3. damage or loss
   4. termination conditions
   5. options to purchase or renew
   6. obsolescence
F. What are the trade-offs among:
   1. sales
   2. fixtures, furniture, machinery and equipment alternatives
   3. fixed and working capital required, annual costs plus cost risk factors

Group VII. *Requirements for Layout and Flow Plan*

A. What layout and flow plan for fixtures, furniture, machinery, equipment, inventory and employees maximizes efficiency in:
   1. facility renovations required
   2. inventory storage and movement
   3. fixtures, furniture, machinery and equipment installation, maintenance and repair
   4. utilities use
   5. employees required
   6. production or service per piece of equipment and man hour

THE BUSINESS PLAN RESEARCH AND PLANNING GUIDE 117

   7. safety
   8. display access
   9. production, sales or service supervision
   10. production, sales and/or service process flexibility
   11. working conditions conducive to employee satisfaction
   12. shopping conditions conducive to customer purchases
   13. security
   14. management
   15. administration
   16. capacity expansion potential
 B. What layout and flow plan features are required by:
   1. federal and state labor practices and safety laws
   2. state and local health, sanitation, fire and building codes
 C. What are the trade-offs among efficiency factors identified?
 D. What are the trade-offs among:
   1. sales
   2. costs
   3. layout and flow plan efficiency

Group VIII. Costs of Developing and Installing Layout and Flow Plan

 A. Assuming that each layout and flow plan option is open, how do feasible alternatives compare in:
   1. total fixed and working capital required
   2. facility renovations costs
   3. installation, maintenance and repair costs
   4. utilities costs
   5. labor, supervisory force and personnel costs
   6. security costs
   7. insurance costs
   8. total effect on monthly and annual net income and cash flow
   9. capacity expansion costs
 B. What are the trade-offs among:
   1. sales
   2. layout and flow plan alternatives
   3. initial and annual fixed and working capital required

2) PERSONNEL AND PROFESSIONAL SERVICES PLAN

Group I. Requirements for Labor and Supervisory Force

A. What production, sales or service functions must employees perform?

B. What performance levels must workers reach for each function per hour, week, month and year?

C. What physical and mental capacities, skills and experience must workers have to attain these performance levels?

D. How do workers capacities, skills and experience alternatives compare in:
   1. numbers required
   2. productivity
   3. flexibility
   4. reliability
   5. capacity expansion potential

E. What functions must supervisors perform?

F. For how many production, sales or service functions and workers must each supervisor plan, schedule, make task assignments and take responsibility?

G. What physical and mental capacities, skills and experience must supervisors have to perform at the required level?

H. How do supervisor capacities, skills and experience alternatives compare in:
   1. numbers required
   2. labor productivity created
   3. labor efficiency created
   4. flexibility
   5. sales continuity created
   6. capacity expansion potential

I. What are the trade-offs among:
   1. sales
   2. worker capacities, skills and experience
   3. supervisor capacities, skills and experience

Group II. Availability of Labor

A. What is the *labor market area?* What distance can workers and supervisors be expected to travel to work?

B. What capacities, skills and experience are available in the labor market area? Can workers and supervisors with the desired

THE BUSINESS PLAN RESEARCH AND PLANNING GUIDE 119

   capacities, skills and experience be located and recruited? Where? How?
C. If not, can trainable persons be located and recruited? Where? How?
D. Once they are recruited:
   1. What training is required?
   2. Who can train?
   3. What training time is required?
   4. Is training required before the business opens, on the job or both?

Group III. Costs of Labor
A. Is it better to pay workers and supervisors:
   1. hourly or weekly wages
   2. a weekly, monthly or yearly salary
   3. wages plus production or sales bonuses
   4. salary plus production or sales bonuses
   5. salary plus a percentage of sales
   6. piece-work rates plus production bonuses
B. Federal, state and occasionally municipal laws govern overtime bases. If labor requirements vary seasonally, should the business hire additional employees or pay overtime to the existing employees?
C. Is it better to provide fringe benefits, higher basic compensation or neither? If fringe benefits are provided, which benefits are appropriate for the business and the recipients?
D. Is some form of profit-sharing practical and desirable?
E. Is it better to pay trainees on the same basis and at the same rate as regular employees? Is it better to provide trainees with the same fringe benefits as regular employees?
F. Can the business obtain government grants or contract funds to subsidize the cost of training and employing trainees? Do the administrative time and costs connected with such funds make subsidizing economical?
G. Assuming the each compensation plan option is open, how do feasible labor and supervisory force requirement alternatives compare in:
   1. total working capital required
   2. basic compensation cost per month and year
   3. payroll tax and fringe benefit cost per month and year
   4. total effect on monthly and annual net income and cash flow
   5. capacity expansion costs

H. What are the trade-offs among:
  1. sales
  2. numbers, capacities, skills and experience of workers and supervisors
  3. working capital required plus annual compensation, payroll tax and fringe benefit costs

Group IV. Requirements for Management and Administrative Personnel

A. What managerial and administrative functions must personnel perform?
B. Does the business require in-house capability to:
  1. do marketing (develop customers, contracts, sales)
  2. research, develop or design new products
  3. project sales and budget expenditures
  4. price goods, merchandise or services
  5. bid for contracts
  6. design merchandise displays
  7. plan advertising and promotion
  8. purchase inventory
  9. control inventory
  10. hire, orient and train employees
  11. design and/or control production, sales or service processes
  12. control overhead
  13. create and administer cost accounting and control systems
  14. do bookkeeping
  15. create and administer payroll and fringe benefits payment systems
  16. create and administer real estate, sales, federal and state withholding, social security (FICA) and payroll tax payments systems
  17. develop periodic income statements and balance sheets
  18. analyze income and budgets
  19. manage business finances
  20. prepare federal and state income tax returns
C. What performance standards must personnel meet for each function?
D. What technical competence, skills and experience must personnel have to meet these performance standards?
E. How do competence, skills and experience alternatives compare in:
  1. numbers required

2. productivity
3. flexibility
4. supplemental professional services and technical assistance needed
5. capacity expansion potential

F. Which required functions can the manager perform? What technical competence, skill and experience does he/she have? In which functional areas can he make the most significant and efficient contribution? How much can he do?

G. How do personnel and the manager's competence, skills and experience alternatives compare in:
   1. numbers required
   2. productivity
   3. flexibility
   4. supplemental professional services and technical assistance needed
   5. capacity expansion potential

H. What are the trade-offs among:
   1. sales
   2. personnel competence, skills and experience
   3. the manager's competence, skills and experience

I. What is the labor market area? What distance can personnel be expected to move for employment or travel to work?

Group V. Availability of Management and Administrative Personnel

A. What technical competence, skills and experience are available in the labor market area? Can personnel with the desired competence, skills and experience be located and recruited? Where? How?

B. If not, can trainable persons be located and recruited? Where? How?

C. Once they are recruited:
   1. What training is required?
   2. Who can train?
   3. What training time is required?
   4. Is training required before the business opens, on the job or both?

Group VI. Costs of Management and Administrative Personnel

A. Is it better to pay management and administrative personnel:
   1. hourly or weekly wages
   2. a weekly, monthly or yearly salary
   3. wages plus production or sales bonuses

4. salary plus production or sales bonuses

5. salary plus a percentage of sales

B. Is it better to pay overtime? If overtime is paid, what basis is best for payment?

C. Is it better to provide fringe benefits, higher basic compensation or neither? If fringe benefits are provided, which benefits are appropriate for the business and the recipients?

D. Is some form of profit-sharing practical and desirable?

E. Is it better to pay trainees on the same basis and at the same rate as regular personnel? Is it better to provide trainees with the same fringe benefits as regular personnel?

F. How much will the manager draw from the business? How will he/she draw it?

G. Assuming that each compensation plan option is open, how do feasible management and administrative personnel alternatives compare in:

1. total dollars required

2. basic compensation cost per month and year

3. payroll tax and fringe benefits costs per month and year

4. supplemental professional service and technical assistance costs per month and year

5. total effect on monthly and annual net income and cash flow

6. capacity expansion costs

H. What are the trade-offs among:

1. sales

2. numbers, competence, skills and experience of management and administrative personnel

3. working capital required plus annual compensation, payroll tax, fringe benefit and professional services and technical assistance costs

Group VII. Requirements for Professional Services and Technical Assistance

A. What professional service and technical assistance functions must independent personnel perform for the business?

B. Does the business require professional services or technical assistance in the areas of:

1. marketing

2. new products research development and design

3. sales projection and budgeting

4. pricing and/or bidding
5. merchandise display
6. advertising and promotion
7. inventory purchasing
8. employee training
9. cost accounting and control system creation and administration
10. book and record keeping system creation and administration
11. payroll, fringe benefit and all tax payment systems creation and administration
12. income statement and balance sheet development
13. income and budget analysis
14. finance management
15. income tax return preparation

C. Does the business require a lawyer or law firm to:
1. draw up and file partnership papers and agreements or incorporation papers, articles of incorporation and by-laws
2. assure compliance with federal, state and local partnership, corporation, securities, tax and other laws and regulations governing conduct of the business
3. negotiate and draw up any purchase and sale agreements, leases, lease/purchase agreements, contracts or other legal documents binding the business
4. apply for local government licenses and permits necessary to do business
5. in general represent the business

D. What are the in-house versus independent professional and technical capability trade-offs among the functions identified?

E. What are the trade-offs between sales and in-house versus independent capability alternatives?

Group VIII. Costs of Professional Services and Technical Assistance

A. Is it better to pay professionals and technical assistance resources:
1. an hourly rate
2. a monthly or annual retainer
3. a percentage of sales
4. by task
5. some combination of the above

B. What amount should the business pay?

C. Assuming that each compensation option is open, how do feasible professional service and technical assistance alternatives compare in:
   1. fixed and working capital required
   2. professional services and technical assistance alternatives
   3. fixed and working capital required plus annual costs?

FINANCIAL ANALYSIS

The financial analysis helps organize and analyze all the sales estimates and cost data developed in the market analysis, the product and sales assessment and the technical and operational plan. The financial analysis answers the question: Is the business financially feasible? It evaluates whether sales income is enough to justify the financial investment and cover the costs involved in opening and operating the business.

Financial plans will normally include:
- a statement of financial requirements
- an income statement
- a cash flow analysis
- a break-even analysis
- a balance sheet

Statement of Financial Requirements

The Statement of Financial Requirements outlines the financial outlays, expenditures and reserves necessary to begin business and the projected sources of financing for these requirements. Start-up requirements include funds for purchasing fixed assets, prepaid items and deposits, pre-opening expenses, purchasing inventory and supplies, plus the dollars needed for working capital (see Figure 14.1). You may find it easier to look at total sources and total uses of funds. Such a format is shown in Figure 14.2.

A statement of financial requirements shows the assets the business must purchase, the prepayments and deposits the business must make, the pre-opening expenses the business must pay and the working capital the business must have on hand before it begins operations. The statement also shows where the business expects to obtain the funds needed.

Income Statement

A pro forma income statement predicts how profitable a business will be. It shows how much money a business cleared or will clear over a given period of time.

Generally, if the pro forma income statement does not predict sufficient annual profit, the business should not be started. On the other hand, it may be possible to restructure the business package so as to produce an

FIGURE 14.1: Analysis of Financial Requirements

Analysis of Financial Requirements
Sources and Uses of Funds

ITEM	FUNDS REQUIRED	SOURCE OF FUNDS		
	Total	Provided by owner	To be financed	Source of financing*
FIXED ASSETS Automotive Equipment Machinery and Equipment Fixtures and Furniture Real Estate Leasehold Improvements Other Organizational Expenses** Sub Total	$	$	$	$
PREPAID ITEMS AND DEPOSITS Rent Deposit Utilities Deposit Insurance Taxes, Licenses and Fees Telephone Deposit Rent/Mortgage Payment Other Sub Total	$	$	$	$
PRE-OPENING EXPENSES Office Supplies Utilities Insurance Product Testing Personnel Advertising and Promotion Training Other Sub Total	$	$	$	$
INVENTORY AND SUPPLIES	$	$	$	$
WORKING CAPITAL (Cash Flow)				
OTHER				
Contingency Fund	$	$	$	$
TOTAL				

 *Debt, equity, grant, donation and from whom (supplier, bank, corporation, foundation, government, etc.

 **Organizational expenses equal the accounting and legal fees necessary to start, expand or acquire the business. They are considered an asset until the business opens. After the business opens, they are written off or "expenses."

FIGURE 14.2: Sources and Uses of Funds

Sources

1. Term loan $_____
2. Mortgage loan $_____
3. Guaranteed bank loan $_____
4. New equity investment $_____
5. Loan from supplier $_____
    Total $_____

Uses

1. Purchase property $_____
2. Equipment $_____
3. Renovations $_____
4. Inventory $_____
5. Working capital $_____
6. Organizational expenses $_____
7. Pre-opening expenses $_____
8. Prepaid items $_____
9. Cash reserve for contingencies $_____
    Total $_____

adequate level of return. Restructuring amounts either to expanding sales or reducing expenses. Expanding sales might involve changing the product, labor force, location, customers or customer services. Reducing expenses might entail cutting the labor force, salaries and wages, rent or customer services. At some point the restructuring process results in a new and different business.

Most sources of financing require pro forma income statements for the first three years of operation. Second- and third-year projections are reasoned extensions of first-year figures. As sales volume increases, the expenses tied to generating sales also increase. However, expenses do not always grow at the same rate as sales. Some costs of doing business remain fixed or change very little. For example, in most manufacturing businesses, payroll grows at a rate similar to sales, but office expenses and the cost of professional services do not. In most retail businesses advertising and promotional expenses vary directly with sales, but payroll and rent rise at a much slower rate.

In addition to the three annual projections, the business should project income statements for each of the first twelve months. Doing monthly calculations clarifies the relationship between sales and variable expenses, and sales and fixed expenses (see Figure 14.3). Another sample income statement can be found in Chapter 11.

Cash Flow Analysis

A cash flow analysis shows how much of the cash generated by the business remains after both expenses (including interest) and principal repayment on financing are paid. A projected cash flow indicates whether the business will have cash to pay its expenses and loans and make a profit. The business should project annual cash flows for the first three years of operation and monthly cash flows for the first year of operation. The analyses are crucial in determining if the business can operate without additional cash injections, or when and how much cash will be required to continue operation.

To do a cash flow analysis, remember:

1. Depreciation is a non-cash expense and should not be subtracted as an expense when analyzing cash flow. Add depreciation and net profit to find cash generated.

2. Principal repayments must be added to total cash expenditures. Only interest payments are included on the income statement.

3. Track the timing of cash receipts and disbursements. A purchase that was charged may not become cash for thirty or sixty days. Also, you may be able to delay payment on certain items for a similar period of time. If upon analysis the net cash flow is a negative number, the business does not have sufficient cash to cover its expenses and repay its loan. If the net cash flow is a positive number, it should be examined to determine whether it represents sufficient cash return to the owner as well as sufficient reinvestment funds needed to make the business grow and achieve a projected sales potential.

A sample cash flow analysis can be found in Chapter 11.

Balance Sheet

A balance sheet shows a businesses' assets, liabilities and net worth at a given point in time. An opening balance sheet describes the financial status of the business the day before it opens. Some financing sources wish to see projected balance sheets for each quarter of the first year and annually for the next two years.

Half of the balance sheet lists assets; the other half lists liabilities and equities. Assets equal liabilities plus equities. Liabilities are usually divided into two categories: current and long term. Current liabilities are those debts that the business owes within the first year of operation; long-term liabilities are debts that the business owes over an extended period of time.

FIGURE 14.3: Sample Income Statement

_____	Sales or Gross Receipts		$_____
	Beginning Inventory	$_____	
	Inventory Purchased/Manufactured	_____	
	Less Ending Inventory	_____	
	Cost of Goods Sold*		$_____
_____	Gross Profit**		$_____
_____	Less Business Expenses		
	Rent	_____	
	Depreciation***	_____	
	Repairs	_____	
	Salaries and Wages	_____	
	Payroll Taxes and Fringe Benefits	_____	
	Taxes, Licenses, and Fees	_____	
	Insurance	_____	
	Accounting, Legal and Professional Fees	_____	
	Bad Debts	_____	
	Telephone	_____	
	Utilities	_____	
	Supplies	_____	
	Security	_____	
	Auto and Truck	_____	
	Advertising and Promotion	_____	
	Interest	_____	
	Miscellaneous	_____	
	Total Expenses		$_____
_____	Net Profit Before Taxes		$_____
_____	Federal Income Taxes (Corporation Only)		$_____
_____	Net Profit		$_____

*Includes finished product or raw materials, labor and overhead costs directly attributed to the manufacturing or production of the product or service to be sold. Waste or pilferage is included in this cost.

**Gross profit equals "sales" minus the "cost of goods sold." The figure that remains is the income available to cover business expenses and produce a profit.

***Depreciation is a non-cash expense, and as such, it does not require paying over out-of-pocket cash. Furniture, fixtures and equipment are examples of depreciable assets. It is possible to calculate and fix standards for how long an asset will take to depreciate. This time period is known as the "useful life" of the asset. Using the depreciation concept, a business may write off or "expense" the purchase price of the asset over its useful life.

The business pays for the asset only once at the beginning of its useful life. However, the asset loses some of its original value each day of every year in that life. This value loss is considered a cost, or expense, of doing business. Thus, a business may treat depreciation as an expense even though it does not entail spending cash. The depreciation amount written off generally equals the cost of the asset divided by the number of years in its useful life divided by the time period covered in the statement.

All balance sheets are presented in exactly the same format (see Figure 14.4). Do not deviate from it. A sample opening balance sheet is shown in Figure 14.5.

Description of Major Balance Sheet Categories

- *Current assets:* cash and cash substitutes, such as bonds, government notes, accounts receivable, notes receivable, inventory and prepaid expenses.
- *Fixed assets:* land, plant, buildings, leasehold improvements, equipment, vehicles, fixtures and furniture. Fixed assets with limited life are depreciated. Cost minus depreciation = fixed asset value.
- *Other assets:* patents, copyrights, notes receivable from officers and employees, exclusive use of contracts.
- *Current liabilities:* accounts payable, notes payable, accrued expenses, taxes payable, current portion of long-term debt, and other obligations due within one year.
- *Long-term liabilities:* mortgages, bank loans and equipment loans (minus current portion of long-term debt).
- *Net worth:* owner's equity, retained earnings, other equity.
- *Footnotes:* any extraordinary items, one-time expenses, contingent liabilities (such as law suits or audits) and changes in accounting practices.

FIGURE 14.4: Basic Balance Sheet Format

ASSETS

Current Assets		$_____
Fixed Assets	$_____	
Less Accumulated Depreciation	$_____	
Net Fixed Assets		$_____
Other Assets		$_____
TOTAL ASSETS		$_____

Footnotes:

LIABILITIES

Current Liabilities	$_____
Long-term Liabilities	$_____
TOTAL LIABILITIES	$_____
Net Worth (total assets minus total liabilities) or Owner's Equity	$_____
TOTAL LIABILITIES AND NET WORTH	$_____

Footnotes:

FIGURE 14.5: Sample Balance Sheet

Name of Business
Balance Sheet
Date

ASSETS		LIABILITIES	
Current Assets		Current Liabilities	
Cash	$2,000	Accounts Payable	$8,000
Accounts Receivable (Net)	$1,500	Current Portion of Long-term Debt	$1,500
Merchandise Inventory	$4,000		
Supplies	$500	Total Current Liabilities	$9,500
Prepaid Expenses	$300	Long-term Liabilities	
Total Current Assets	$8,300	Note Payable	$500
Fixed Assets		Bank Loan Payable	$1,500
Fixtures and Leasehold Improvements	$15,000	Equity Loan Payable	$10,000
		Total Lng-trm Liabilities	$12,000
Building/Real Estate	$5,000	Total Liabilities	21,500
Machinery/Equipment	$3,000	NET WORTH	
Vehicles	$6,000	Owner's Equity	$15,800
Total Fixed Assets	$29,000	Total Liabilities and Net Worth	$37,300
Total Assets	$37,300		

Break-even Analysis

The break-even point is the level of sales that generates neither a positive nor a negative net cash flow after interest and principal payments have been made. In other words, when a business breaks even, it has a zero net cash flow. The break-even point can be expressed either in dollars or in unit sales. Remember that increased sales do not necessarily mean increased profits.

To do a break-even analysis you must first determine:

1. All fixed cash costs. Fixed costs are those that do not vary according to sales. Add the dollar figures for all fixed costs to obtain a total. Include interest, amortization and depreciation.

2. All variable cash costs. The cost of goods sold is one of the chief variable cash costs. Variable costs are those that change in proportion to variations in sales. As such, every variable cost may be expressed as a percentage of sales. Figure out what percentage of sales each variable cost is. Add the percentages figures to obtain a total percentage of sales for variable costs.

The basic break-even formula is

$$S = FC + VC$$

where

S = break-even level of sales,
FC = fixed costs in dollars and
VC = variable costs in dollars

If you want to calculate a break-even in dollars and therefore do not know total variable costs, a variation of the formula is used. If you know what gross margin to expect as a percent of sales, use the formula:

$$S = \frac{FC}{GM}$$

where

GM = gross margin expressed as a percent of sales.

To calculate a break-even in terms of the number of units you need to sell, divide the break-even derived above in dollars by the unit price. This will give you the number of units that must be sold.

For example, if your income statement includes

Total sales = $215,000
Gross margin = $ 58,000

and you calculate fixed costs to be $61,000, gross margin expressed as a percentage of total sales will be

$$\frac{58{,}000}{215{,}000} = 27\%$$

$$\text{Break-even} = S = \frac{FC}{GM} = \frac{61{,}000}{.27} = \$225{,}926/\text{year}$$

15 PARTING ADVICE

Operating the business venture is a subject for another time. But in closing, the following miscellaneous advice is offered:

- During the early operating stage, the business will focus on marketing and sales. At the same time, however, the business must build its production capacity to meet the demand it is creating. The organization might want to subcontract certain aspects of the operation until such time as it has the capacity to manage all aspects of the business simultaneously. It is important that the subcontractor meet the same quality standards established for the business.
- If the business plan anticipates expansion in the near future, the organization should consider hiring for growth—hiring a comptroller instead of a bookkeeper, for example, or employing an operations manager rather than a foreman. The presence of experienced and skilled staff in the early years can accelerate business growth and position the business to take advantage of that growth. Businesses that start small often stay small because they are unprepared for growth.
- The nonprofit should take the time and spend the money to hire good management. Whether the manager comes from inside or outside of the existing organization, he or she is key to the success of the business. It is the manager who makes the day-to-day decisions that set the tone and direction for the venture.
- The organization should understand that management might change two or three times before the right manager is found.

- The nonprofit must be prepared for the time when additional capital investment is required by the growing business. Board and staff members may well resist a second round of fundraising. However, if they are aware of the positive nature of this eventuality, they are more likely to support the need for more financing.
- The nonprofit must be prepared to admit when it has a losing venture. In the same way that there can be resistance to additional investment in a successful venture, there can be reluctance to abandon a failing business. The organization must evaluate its venture honestly and, if it is a loser, cut its losses.
- Stay close to your customers through constant feedback. The business that is responsive to the needs of its consumers also learns about new product ideas and second-generation ideas that evolve naturally from the original business idea.
- The nonprofit's board and staff members will get nervous from time to time. Their personal and institutional conservatism may surface in a movement to abandon the business venture. Reassurance, based on the venture's goals, business plan and progress toward milestones, is essential at such times.
- Key players should be informed about the venture's successes as well as its problems. However, the organization must limit outside involvement in the day-to-day details of the operation. Too much outside involvement is interference and can cripple management, making it impossible to run the business.
- The nonprofit must be ready to learn from its mistakes, for mistakes will surely be made. This learning should be positive, not punitive. The organization should admit the mistake, understand what went wrong and take action to prevent the same mistake from happening again.
- The business must prepare for cash flow problems by establishing a working relationship with its suppliers and bank to help during these rough periods.
- The organization should be prepared to learn: marketing will take more time and more money than expected; sales will develop more slowly than expected; and cash will be received much more slowly than expected.
- Creative resource-tapping provides the business venture with needed support and free advice. But the nonprofit must recognize when to invest in the right information

from the right expert. A small investment in a lawyer's, accountant's or consultant's services may spell the difference between business success and business failure.

In embarking on a business venture, the nonprofit organization must expect to invest a lot of time, energy and good will. The nonprofit will discover that its business adventure pays off in kind and in independence.

BIBLIOGRAPHY

The following list of publications was compiled to assist nonprofit organizations in developing business skills. It is not meant to be an exhaustive list of publications on business start-ups. Consult your local library or bookstore for additional resource materials as well as the U.S. Small Business Administration, U.S. Department of Commerce, banks, accounting firms, state and local agencies and business schools.

VENTURING

The Complete Guide to Money Making Ventures for Nonprofit Organizations. Peter C. Brown, 1986.
   The Taft Group
   5130 MacArthur Boulevard, NW
   Washington, DC 20016
   800-424-3761

Stepping Out into the Marketplace: The Pitfalls of Earned Income for the Small Non-Profits. January, 1986.
   Community Resource Exchange
   17 Murray Street, 4th Floor
   New York, NY 10007

Enterprise in the Nonprofit Sector. James Crimmins and Mary Keil, 1983.
   Partners for Livable Places
   1429 21st Street, NW
   Washington, DC 20036
   202-887-5990

Filthy Rich and Other Nonprofit Fantasies, Richard Steckel, 1988.
   Ten Speed Press
   P.O. Box 7123
   Berkeley, CA 94707

Looking at Income Generating Businesses for Small Nonprofit Organizations, William Duncan, July 1982.
>Center for Community Change
Publications Department
1000 Washington Avenue, NW
Washington, DC 20007

Managing for Profit in a Nonprofit World, Paul B. Firstenberg, 1986.
>The Foundation Center
79 Fifth Avenue
New York, NY

New Venture Creation: A Guide to Entrepreneurship (second edition) Jeffry A. Timmons, 1985.
>Richard D. Irwin, Inc.
1818 Ridge Road
Homewood, IL 60430

"The Nonprofits Business: Battling the Bottom Line," three-part series, *The Washington Post,* November 24, 25, 26, 1985.

"The Nonprofits Drop the 'Non.'" *The New York Times,* November 24, 1985.

The Nonprofit Entrepreneur: Creating Ventures to Earn Income, edited by Edward Skloot, 1988.
>The Foundation Center
79 Fifth Avenue
New York, NY

Non-profit Piggy Goes to Market, Robin Simons, Lisa Farber Miller, Peter Lansfelder, 1984.
>The Children's Museum of Denver
2121 Crescent Drive
Denver, CO 80211

Profit for Nonprofits—Myth or Reality: A manual on income generation for voluntary human service agencies, 1985.
>Greater NY Fund/United Way
99 Park Avenue
New York, NY 10016
212-557-1050

Profit Making by Non-Profits, Bruce Hopkins, 1982.
>The Grantsmanship Center
650 South Spring Street, Suite 507
Los Angeles, CA 90014
213-689-9222

"Should Not-for-Profits Go Into Business," Edward Skloot, *Harvard Business Review,* Jan./Feb. 1983.

A Step Toward Independence: Economic Self-Sufficiency, edited by Janice Moore, 1986.
>National Coalition Against Domestic Violence
>Suite 305
>2401 Virginia Avenue, NW
>Washington, DC 20037

BUSINESS PLANNING AND MANAGEMENT

The Business Planning Guide: Creating a Plan for Success in Your Own Business. David H. Bangs, Jr.
>Upstart Publishing Company
>P.O. Box 323
>Portsmouth, NH 03801

Business Spin-offs: Planning the Organizational Structure of Business Activities: A manual for not-for-profit organizations, 1982.
>Center for Urban Economic Development
>815 West Van Buren, Suite 500
>Chicago, IL 60607

Casebook of Management for Nonprofit Organizations: Entrepreneurship and Organizational Change in the Human Services, Denis R. Young, 1985.
>Haworth Press
>28 East 22nd Street
>New York, NY 10016-6194

The Entrepreneur's Guide to Planning a Business: How to Think Through Your Business and Then Write a Business Plan. James R. Ball, 1986.
>EntreGuide Publications, Inc.
>2911 Hunter Mill Road, #200
>P.O. Box 434
>Oakton, VA 22124

Growing a Business, Paul Hawkin, 1987.
>Simon & Schuster
>1230 Avenue of the Americas
>New York, NY 10030

Nonprofit Management: A Report on Current Research and Areas for Development. (paper no. 108) Melissa Middleton
>Program on Non-Profit Organizations
>Institute for Social & Policy Studies
>Yale University
>154 Yale Station
>New Haven, CT 06520

Nonprofit World, a magazine published six times/year by the Society for Nonprofit Organizations. Includes articles on entrepreneurship, marketing and tax and legal issues.
> The Society for Nonprofit Organizations
> 6314 Odana Road, Suite 1
> Madison, WI 53719

Your Business: A Management Guide for Small Business
> New York State Department of Commerce
> Division of Small Business
> 230 Park Avenue
> New York, NY 10169

UNFAIR COMPETITION

Issue Alert: Unfair Competition with Small Business. August 1986.
> Office of Advocacy
> U.S. Small Business Administration
> Washington, DC
> 202-634-7600

Shifting the Debate: Public/Private Sector Relations in the Modern Welfare State, Susan Ostrander, Stuart Langton and Jan Varntil, 1987
> Transaction Books
> Rutgers University
> New Brunswick, NJ 08903

Unfair Competition: The Challenge to Charitable Tax Exemption, W. Harrison Wellford and Janne G. Gallagher, 1988
> The National Assembly of National Voluntary Health and Social Welfare Organizations
> 1319 F Street, NW
> Washington, DC 20004

Unfair Competition in the States: A Report for State Business Leaders on How to Combat Competition for Non-profit Business Ventures, July 1985.
> Business Coalition for Fair Competition
> 1725 K Street, NW, Suite 301
> Washington, DC
> 202-887-5872

TAX AND LEGAL ISSUES

Business and the Non-profit: Tax and Legal Implementation, Dr. Thomas Jones, 1986.
> Enterprise Fund, Inc.
> P.O. Box 98
> Churchton, MD 20783

The Non-Profit Council, a newsletter on tax and legal issues.
   Bruce Hopkins
   c/o Charitable Productions Co. Inc.
   P.O. Box 40727, NW
   Washington, DC 20016

Also see: Business Spinoffs and The Complete Guide to Money Making Ventures for Nonprofit Organizations, listed above.

MARKETING

Marketing for Nonprofit Organizations, Philip Kotler, 1982.
   Prentice-Hall, Inc.
   Englewood Cliffs, NJ 07632
   201-767-5049

"Non-Profits: Check your Attention to Customers," Alan R. Anderson, *Harvard Business Review,* May, June 1982.

ABOUT THE AMERICAN COUNCIL FOR THE ARTS

The American Council for the Arts (ACA) is one of the nation's primary sources of legislative news affecting all of the arts and serves as a leading advisor to arts administrators, educators, elected officials, arts patrons and the general public. To accomplish its goal of strong advocacy of the arts, ACA promotes public debate in various national, state and local forums; communicates as a publisher of books, journals, *Vantage Point* magazine and *ACA UpDate*; provides information services through its extensive arts education, policy and management library; and has as its key policy issues arts education, the needs of individual artists, private-sector initiatives, and international cultural relations.

BOARD OF DIRECTORS

Chairman
Gerald D. Blatherwick

President
Milton Rhodes

Vice Chairmen
Mrs. Jack S. Blanton, Sr.
Toni K. Goodale
Howard S. Kelberg
Donald R. Greene

Secretary
Fred Lazarus IV

Treasurer
Patrick W. Kenny

Past Chairmen
Eugene C. Dorsey
Donald G. Conrad
Marshall S. Cogan
Louis Harris
David Rockefeller, Jr.
George M. Irwin

Members
Judith F. Baca
John Paul Batiste
Harry Belafonte
Madeleine Berman
Theodore Bikel
Willard L. Boyd

Ernest L. Boyer
John Brademas
Mrs. Martin Brown
Mrs. D. Wayne Calloway
Nedda Casei
Terri Childs
Ronald E. Compton
Donald G. Conrad
John Crosby
Colleen Dewhurst
Eugene C. Dorsey
Sunny Dupree, Esq.
Stephanie French
John Galvin
Yolanda O. Garcia
Jack Golodner
Eldridge C. Hanes
David H. Harris
Daniel Herrick
David S. Hershberg
Richard Hunt
Henry E. Kates
Jonathan Katz
Howard S. Kelberg
John Kilpatrick
Frank W. Lynch
John J. Mahlmann
Bruce Marks
Timothy J. McClimon
James M. McClymond
Lee Kimche-McGrath

Henry Moran
Velma Morrison
Sondra G. Myers
Mrs. Charles D. Peebler
Murray Charles Pfister
Janis Provisor
Mrs. Richard S.
 Reynolds III
W. Ann Reynolds
Mrs. Paul Schorr III
Gerard Schwarz
Mrs. Alfred R. Shands III
Mrs. David E. Skinner
Kathy D. Southern
Elton B. Stephens
John Straus
Roselyne C. Swig
William Taylor
Allen M. Turner
Esther Wachtell
Vivian M. Warfield
Mrs. Gerald H. Westby
Arthur Whitelaw
Mrs. Pete Wilson
Masaru Yokouchi

Legal Counsel
Howard S. Kelberg

Special Counsel
Jack G. Duncan

ABOUT THE AUTHOR

LAURA LANDY is President of Entrepreneurship Training & Consulting, Inc. and Director of the Initiative on Nonprofit Entrepreneurship (I.N.E.) at New York University's Stern School of Business Administration's Center for Entrepreneurial Studies. Both organizations specialize in the entrepreneurial and market activities of nonprofits. Ms. Landy has trained more than 1,500 individuals across the country in the art of business venture planning. She has degrees from Washington University in St. Louis, the University of California-Berkeley, and an MBA from New York University.